*Praise for*

# WHY KIDS LOVE (AND HATE) SCHOOL
## Reflections on Practice

"*Why Kids Love (and Hate) School: Reflections on Practice* is a tonic book for the Age of Inequality. The authors give us a sparkling collection of stories and images, crisp essays, worthy examples and counterexamples of love and learning from across the world. Their moving portraits of loved schools and hated schools got me to question what I thought I knew for sure about kids, to listen more and talk less, and to see schooling once again through the eyes of schoolchildren."

—CHRISTOPHER M. CLARK, MICHIGAN STATE UNIVERSITY

"*Why Kids Love (and Hate) School: Reflections on Practice* reveals how to make school more engaging, intellectually enriching, uplifting, and fun. For teachers and administrators who want their students to flourish, *Why Kids Love (and Hate) School* is a must-read."

—LAWRENCE BAINES, UNIVERSITY OF OKLAHOMA

# THE ACADEMY FOR EDUCATIONAL STUDIES BOOK SERIES

## Steven P. Jones and Eric C. Sheffield, *Editors*

*The Academy for Educational Studies Book Series* focuses serious attention on the often-missed nexus of educational theory and educational practice. The volumes in this series, both monographs and edited collections, consider theoretical, philosophical, historical, sociological, and other conceptual orientations in light of what those orientations can tell readers about successful classroom practice and sound educational policy. In this regard, *The Academy for Educational Studies Book Series* aims to offer a wide array of themes, including school reform, content-specific practice, contemporary problems in higher education, the impact of technology on teaching and learning, matters of diversity, and other essential contemporary issues in educational thought and practice.

## BOOKS IN THE SERIES

*Why Kids Love (and Hate) School: Reflections on Difference*

*Why Kids Love (and Hate) School: Reflections on Practice*

**Steven P. Jones** is a professor in the College of Education at Missouri State University and executive director of the Academy for Educational Studies. He is author of *Blame Teachers: The Emotional Reasons for Educational Reform*—a book that investigates how and why so many people try to justify educational change by deriding the efforts and effectiveness of our public school teachers. A former high school English teacher in Jefferson County, Colorado, Jones received his BA in English from the University of Denver, his MA in educational administration from the University of Colorado (Boulder), and his PhD in curriculum and instruction from the University of Chicago.

**Eric C. Sheffield** is professor and department chair of educational studies at Western Illinois University in Macomb. He is also founding editor of the Academy for Educational Studies' peer-reviewed journal, *Critical Questions in Education*. A former English teacher in Putman County, Florida, Sheffield received his BA in philosophy from Illinois College, and his MEd and PhD from the University of Florida.

---

The editors of *The Academy for Educational Studies Book Series* are interested in reviewing manuscripts and proposals for possible publication in the series. Scholars who wish to be considered should email their proposals, along with two sample chapters and current CVs, to the editors. For instructions and advice on preparing a prospectus, please refer to the Myers Education Press website at http://myersed press.com/sites/stylus/MEP/Docs/Prospectus%20Guidelines%20MEP.pdf. You can send your material to:

Steven P. Jones
Eric C. Sheffield
academyedbooks@gmail.com

# WHY KIDS LOVE (AND HATE) SCHOOL

Reflections on Practice

# WHY KIDS LOVE (AND HATE) SCHOOL

Reflections on Practice

Edited by Steven P. Jones and Eric C. Sheffield

Myers
Education
Press

GORHAM, MAINE

Myers
Education
Press

Myers Education Press is an academic publisher specializing in books, e-books, and digital content in the field of education. All of our books are subjected to a rigorous peer-review process and produced in compliance with the standards of the Council on Library and Information Resources.

Library of Congress Cataloging-in-Publication Data available from Library of Congress.

13-digit ISBN 978-1-9755-0099-3 (paperback)
13-digit ISBN 978-1-9755-0098-6 (hard cover)
13-digit ISBN 978-1-9755-0100-6 (library networkable e-edition)
13-digit ISBN 978-1-9755-0101-3 (consumer e-edition)

Printed in the United States of America.

All first editions printed on acid-free paper that meets the American National Standards Institute Z39-48 standard.

Books published by Myers Education Press may be purchased at special quantity discount rates for groups, workshops, training organizations, and classroom usage. Please call our customer service department at 1-800-232-0223 for details.

Cover design by Sophie Appel

Visit us on the web at www.myersedpress.com to browse our complete list of titles.

# CONTENTS

STEVEN P. JONES AND ERIC C. SHEFFIELD

IN OCTOBER 2006, THE Academy for Educational Studies held its second education conference—the first conference in which we decided to invite participants to respond to a particular theme question. The question was short and a little blunt, but we thought it a vital question to ask. The question was: "Why do kids hate school?" The gathering was wonderful, and the discussions were provocative. Since then, the Academy has organized fifteen more conferences, all revolving around one or more theme questions. Now we meet twice a year—once for the Critical Questions in Education Conference, and once for the Critical Questions in Education Symposium (which focuses on a single question).

We invited John Goodlad to speak at that second conference, the one on why kids hate school. Goodlad had to decline our offer. He couldn't come, he said in the message he sent us, because he was recovering from some health issues. But he said more than that in his message. After he explained why he had to decline our offer, he went on to say that, in his opinion, we had asked a bad question. He said we shouldn't be asking why kids "hate" school, because most students *don't* hate school. He said far more students *like* school than hate it, and he urged us to rethink our question.

Well, it was too late to change the question for the conference, but since then we've had a number of years to rethink our approach. We have decided that John Goodlad was right (or we think he was mostly right). And so we have, these many years later, titled this book *Why Kids Love (and Hate) School: Reflections on Practice*. We suppose this title signals something about the two of us doing the editing of this collection—something we would say is true of most human beings: that we listen to and take a lot of advice, even while tending to remain just a little bit stubborn in how we see things. Now the two of us want to say that many students love school, for good reasons, and many students hate school, for good reasons. And those reasons are important to think about. They are especially important for teachers, teachers-to-be, and teacher educators to think about. These are the chief people needing to find ways to secure a hold on the interests, attention, and intentions of the students they do, or will, teach.

But "securing a hold" on student interest or devotion to learning—if that's even the right way to talk about a central task of schooling—is just as tricky to do as it is to talk about. First of all, we have to admit that not every student is going to walk through the school doors every day feeling absolutely on fire about learning. Philip Jackson, in *What Is Education?* (2012), reminds us that not every student is going to love everything put in front of him or her by a teacher (p. 56). Kieran Egan, in *An Imaginative Approach to Teaching* (2005), articulates a similar point of view. "Students don't need a throbbing passion for learning algebra or a swooning joy in learning about punctuation," Egan suggests (p. xii). These ideas supply us with a dose of realism—perhaps welcome relief to the teacher who has convinced herself that she is responsible for having students "love" everything going on in her classroom, but perhaps also disillusionment for the optimist teacher who longs to think of all the possibilities that might await her students if they would but embrace the learning being offered them.

But both Jackson and Egan have more to say than what we have so far reported. It's true, Jackson says, that there are limitations on the enthusiasm of students. Yet Jackson argues that every teacher should aspire to having every school subject *matter*—at least minimally—to every student. And it should matter, he argues, not just for instrumental reasons, such as attaining high grades, or winning the teacher's approval, or even opening doors to higher aspirations. It should matter for *intrinsic* reasons. That is, it must matter to students personally. They need to see some essential part of themselves being made in, or reflected in, the subject matter.

And while teachers don't need to see any obvious "throbbing passion" or "swooning joy" reflected in the faces of their students when those students walk in the doors of the classroom to learn algebra or punctuation, Egan goes on to say that "successful education does require some emotional involvement of the students with the subject matter" (Egan, 2005, p. xii). All knowledge, Egan (2005) says, "is human knowledge and all knowledge is a product of human hopes, fears, and passions. To bring knowledge to life in students' minds we must introduce it to students in the context of human hopes, fears, and passions in which it finds its fullest meaning" (p. xii).

So it would appear that teachers (and those who help them) have some work to do, no matter if we're inclined to bathe students, teachers, and schools in the light of "loving school," or if we're more inclined to cast shadows in the worry that students are "hating school." Teachers have to find ways to make things matter to students, at least minimally, and matter to them intrinsically so that they see some part of themselves in the subject matter. Teachers need to connect students emotionally to what they are learning. Students need to learn that the algebra fact and the punctuation rule are meaningful, that these things emanate from human hopes, fears, and passions that all of us continue to feel. Even when teachers do what Jackson and Egan suggest, students may still not love everything put in front of them, but we're betting that not too many students will turn away from this kind of teaching and learning and declare themselves haters of school.

This book also advances lots of ideas about why kids hate school and how we can get them to love school. It would make sense to read the essays in the order they are here presented.

Elizabeth Hobbs examines what we know to be true—that the teacher is central to whether or not students are going to love or hate school. That's something teachers tend to trumpet when, on our best days, we get students excited to learn, but it's something we are silent about when, on our worst days, we find students sullen and quiet. Barbara J. Mallory and James Davis show how "love" can build invitational cultures that support learning. Barbara Rose takes a look at both sides of the issue—what happens to students when love predominates in the school setting, and what happens when it doesn't.

The next two essays—one by Irene S. LaRoche and Robert W. Maloy, and one by Megan J. Sulsberger—suggest different ways of checking in with students to see how they are doing with what a teacher is trying to teach them. We can't know if students are loving school or hating it unless we look and listen carefully. LaRoche and Maloy show how feedback surveys can improve teaching, and Sulsberger shows us (literally) how we can find out how we're doing with younger students.

The essays by Christopher Beckham, Karla Smart-Morstad and Sara Triggs, and Liang Zhao cast a different light on the same subject. There is no doubt students have to struggle some in order to learn, but is this always such a bad thing? This is the question raised by Beckham and also addressed, in very different ways, in the next two essays. Smart-Morstad and Triggs offer a lovely portrait of what we've all heard about—that northern European nations have schools that know how to do things well. Then again, we've also heard some nightmare stories, and Liang Zhao offers one such story as he narrates the "hate school" scenario that characterizes education throughout China.

In the next three essays, Gary Homana, Kari Dahle-Huff, and Megan Hallissey offer particular analyses about how and why we're doing things wrong and what we can do better. Students can become passionate about their learning, Homana argues, when teachers and school administrators know how to activate genuine civic experiences. Dahle-Huff shows how locally relevant texts and place-based education can reach students, and Hallissey reminds us of the advantages of working with developmentally appropriate practices with younger children.

We chose to place the essay by Todd McCardle, Elizabeth Currin, and Stephanie Schroeder, which discusses the "Opt Out" movement, last in this collection. Maybe that's just residue from our original negative thinking expressed in our 2006 conference question, "Why do kids hate school?"—the question Goodlad chided us about. But if schools aren't doing it right; if schools are still pushing students to hate their experiences there—well, then, opting out is truly an option, at least for some students and families.

This closing essay on the Opt Out movement is something like a book-end essay to the one with which we start the collection—the essay from Elizabeth Hobbs that evokes the positive energy of a "love school" mentality involving the work of teachers. Indeed, the entire collection of essays wobbles back and forth a bit between positive "love school" thinking and the more downcast "hate school" thinking. It seems to us that the truth of the matter of why kids are or are not learning is found in both camps. And so we offer this book to help you think through this most complicated and fascinating matter.

We think there is a lot riding on how we come to think about these things.

### References

Egan, K. (2005). *An imaginative approach to teaching*. San Francisco, CA: Jossey-Bass.

Jackson, P. (2012). *What is education?* Chicago: University of Chicago Press.

# CHAPTER ONE

# HOW YOU TEACH IS WHAT YOU TEACH

Elizabeth Hobbs

Kids want to love school. They do. Certainly, for many students school is the center of their educational *and* social existence. But a student's love/hate relationship with school is complicated. Loving school isn't always the "cool" thing to do. And the reality of this love/hate relationship is that it is significantly impacted by a teacher's own love for learning and school. When describing the spark that ignites their love of school and learning, students will often refer to how energized a teacher becomes when speaking about a favorite book or author, or how passionately a teacher works out a challenging math equation on the board, or how actively a teacher participates in a local social justice rally. Teachers have an incredible power to influence this love and effect positive change in the world. It's exciting. It's terrifying. It's inspiring. It's critical.

## The Reality of This Love/Hate Relationship

Even if they are hesitant to admit it, kids often do love school. School is where kids see their friends each day. School is where kids escape their parents each day. School is where kids develop an understanding of themselves while bobbing and swimming in a sea of other selves. School is where struggles and successes all beautifully boil up around them. School awakens new and exciting passions in kids. School even acts as a safe place for many—it guarantees heat every winter and breakfast every morning.

And yet kids so often complain they hate school. This can be paradoxically true. The fact of the matter is that school harbors all that is equally scary. School is where students face bullies and challenges and uncertainty and failure and broken hearts and missed deadlines and seemingly unfair rules, regulations, and expectations. Who wouldn't be overwhelmed when faced with such daunting issues while trying to make sense of an increasingly confusing adult world? Couple this scary world of school with the pressure to maintain an online social world in which students compare their own personal blooper reels to other students' personal highlight reels, and you have a very uncertain set of hurdles that students face each day. The guidance of supportive, energetic, and passionate teachers is a critical component of school, often for reasons completely separate from the curricular content they teach (Banner & Cannon, 1997; Greene, 1995; Noddings, 2003; Wong & Wong, 1991).

### The Role of the Teacher in Supporting This Relationship

Somewhere students' experience and opinion of school change. They morph. By and large, however, they do not go so far as to be entirely irretrievable. One of the most important aspects of school is that it is where kids learn to navigate our complex and, at times, unsettling world; and, generally speaking, kids are eager to do so with the help of supportive teachers. As youngsters, kids often want to be "bigger" (read: older). With this "big-ness," kids have more opportunities, later curfews, and sometimes fewer restrictions placed on them. In school, kids witness firsthand the experiences of those who are just a bit older than they are, and they long to attain that status. They watch and imitate the bigger kids, and they aspire to be like those bigger kids. However this aspiration does not come without growing pains. In this, kids look to their teachers to lead them through these transitions. How we adults handle stress, new challenges, interactions with others, conflict, exciting news, and so on becomes the model for what it means to be "bigger," or older, for our students.

Kids watch us. They watch us closely. In fact, they watch us so closely that it can be a little unnerving. Years ago, as I was teaching a group of sophomores, I noticed they were staring at me rather quizzically. Thinking I must have spinach in my teeth or something equally embarrassing, I finally stopped to ask them about this. One student eventually said, "You're wearing a necklace. You're generally a bracelet person." Seriously? If our students have the ability to focus so intently on such trivial details, then surely the challenge teachers must embrace is to help them channel this intense focus toward inquiry, exploration, learning, problem solving, and creation.

### How You Teach Is What You Teach

Teaching is an exciting job. Teachers give voice to the voiceless. Teachers stand up for those who cannot stand up for themselves. It is my honor and privilege to work every day to help kids discover and become the people they are to be in life.

Again, kids *want* to like school. I see this every year when I engage my own students in conversations about the learning process. Generally speaking, they fondly remember a time in their young lives when they found school and schoolwork enjoyable. Year after year, my students tell me this shift from loving school to hating school occurs when the work becomes more challenging, less about personal choice, and tied to high-stakes grades.

This brings our murky love/hate conundrum into clearer resolution. Indeed, the formidable task before teachers is thus to model and nurture the love of learning for learning's sake. They must harness it, foster it, and help students struggle with it. When teachers see their role as a call to embody this approach to learning and interaction with the world, it can be very powerful.

We often hear of the myriad roles teachers play for students throughout their day. And, to an extent, this is true. Teachers do wear a number of hats during their time with students. From content specialist to life coach, supportive role model to advocate, mentor to disciplinarian, a teacher helps students navigate challenging situations—sometimes even failure. In short, teachers help students navigate their lives.

I tend to cringe at the use of extended war metaphors to describe teaching and education—and yet I often hear them used. From teachers being on the front lines, in the trenches, with boots on the ground, to working triage in their classrooms, the inherent message embedded within these metaphors is that education is a battle, a war. If we follow this line of thought through to its inevitable end, that also means that there must be winners and losers within this educational construct. I reject this notion wholeheartedly. I find it dangerous and divisive.

Education is not a war to win. Education is a journey to embrace.

It is undeniable that teachers have a tremendous responsibility each day to help kids discover and become the people they are to be in life. In addition to expressing sincere enthusiasm for individual content areas, teachers must harness their power to encourage classrooms based in social justice, nurture classrooms that comprise supportive learning communities, and inspire classrooms that foster students' love and pursuit of learning *not for the grade* but *for the experience of it*. When teachers are passionate about their work, many students will, in turn, be more passionate about their own work.

## Making the Case for the Impassioned Teacher

Who doesn't remember watching movies like *Dead Poets Society*, *Mona Lisa Smile*, *Dangerous Minds*, or *Freedom Writers* and dreaming ever so idealistically that our classroom and impact on students would match that of the Hollywood vision? Many of the preservice teachers with whom I have worked over the years have spoken about their desire to be *that* type of teacher to kids. To have *those* moments in the classroom. To make *that* kind of difference. Certainly, some of my more seasoned colleagues may offer a polite, though perhaps subtly condescending, smile at the rookie teacher who hopes for such idealistic interactions with students. But I love hearing this from preservice teachers. It is precisely this type of excitement and passion that our classrooms and students need. Moreover, it is entirely necessary that teachers begin their careers with these goals—goals like this keep teachers coming back to the classroom day after day, year after year, despite the endless paperwork, meetings, new initiatives, standardized tests, bureaucratic minutiae, and countless other unglamorous elements of teaching—not to mention the constant demonization of the profession in politics and the media.

The reality is this: feelings and emotions are contagious. As teachers, we have incredible power to influence the dynamic and environment of our classrooms. The energy and passion teachers bring to their work each day can make or break a lesson, an activity, or even a child. This can be quite a daunting reality for teachers. Many of the unique responsibilities that come with the job can understandably cause teachers to feel overwhelmed. These responsibilities include listening and responding authentically to student needs; modeling social justice in our interactions with students, colleagues, parents, and other stakeholders; expressing passion and enthusiasm for our content areas; working to maintain happiness in the classroom; fighting political maneuvers to hyperstandardize the school experience, and, instead, to preserve a teacher's status as artist in the classroom.

Banner and Cannon (1997), Eisner (1991), and Greene (1995) argue that it is necessary to view teachers as artists so as to maintain the integrity of the teaching craft. More and more we are seeing efforts to standardize education within the United States, and, unfortunately, this "teacher as artist" distinction can get lost in the science of standardization. These researchers ultimately maintain that teaching is just as much an art as it is a science, and in the blending of the two is where education must live. Greene (1967) argues that this artistic quality in a teacher is paramount to the effectiveness of instruction. When teachers channel their inner artist, their passion for their work will inevitably emerge. Tricarico (2015) asserts that when teaching comes from passion and the heart, it "increase[s] the likelihood [to] experience flow and be 'in the zone'" (p. 12). Teachers who find themselves "in the zone" while channeling their inner artist are also more likely to have happier classrooms. Noddings (2003) maintains that happiness in a classroom is a crucial component of overall learning—it can even lead students to find learning fun. She believes students are willing to do more for teachers who regularly exhibit this care within their classrooms and stresses that "worthwhile fun in the classroom is dependent on the teachers' knowledge and artistry" (p. 244).

Many people struggle with this idea of "fun" in the classroom—especially in a world where it seems that the only thing kids want from the adults in their lives is to be entertained. Of course, it is important for teachers to find a balance with which they are comfortable, as we are not hired to be entertainers. However, there is most definitely an aspect of theatric artistry in an active classroom. When teachers love their content and their jobs, it is possible to make lessons and learning come to life. Obviously, there are days when this is just not possible. Yes, there are teachers in the world who are quite dispassionate about their work. Maybe, in fact, on certain days we all embody this dispassion or at least hear whispers of it from deep within, especially when the overwhelming nature of teaching takes hold. I could list a number of times and ways that it would seem impossible to muster such enthusiasm and happiness—but certainly, there is something to the phrase "fake it 'til you make it." Tricarico (2015) reinforces this notion by noting that students are deeply changed by the experiences they have with their teachers. Teachers create these experiences every day.

Noddings (2003) submits that happiness should absolutely be an aim of education, and when teachers are able to make this happen, they are concerned with "both the quality of present experience and the likely contribution of that experience to future happiness" (p. 251). By extension, she asserts that if students are to be happy, their teachers should also be happy. This classroom environment will encourage kids to "seize their educational opportunities with delight, and they will contribute to the happiness of others" (p. 261). As the path of the educational journey influences our tomorrow, the path is ultimately very important. As such, it "helps to love the path" (Tricarico, 2015, p. 3).

### Not Just an English Thing

I teach English. Have I mentioned that yet? I do. Perhaps the reason I haven't mentioned this rather important element of my job yet is that I see it as only a part of what I do each day. Do I want kids to be able to read and write effectively? Sure. Do I want kids to craft cogent arguments and support each argument with well-documented, credible evidence? Of course. Do I want kids to feel confident speaking in front of an audience, or engaging in academic discourse, or working collaboratively with their peers on large tasks? Without question.

However, there are certain non-negotiables that must be established in my classroom before any of those English things can happen. First and foremost, students need to feel safe in the environment I've created for them. They must feel that I appreciate their presence, contributions, personalities, and imperfections. Sometimes students enter my classroom with negative attitudes toward English—attitudes that have generally been shaped by previous school experiences. In these situations, we first have to work through the muck of these attitudes and experiences before we can move forward with our own learning.

For instance, by the time kids get to high school they will often claim they "hate" to read. However, they did not always hate to read. I know this to be true. There was a time when *every single kid* in my classroom liked reading. I see this every year when I engage my sophomores in a discussion about when they loved to read. During this conversation, they excitedly list picture books, various magazines, Choose Your Own Adventure books, even *Walter the Farting Dog* as reading they remember fondly. The challenge for me is to find ways to tap into this former passion and potentially rekindle some of it during the year.

Learning and schooling are not easy. There are times when I want my students to struggle with their thoughts and the overall experience of learning and creating. The reality is that a teacher's attitude and approach to tough material set the tone for students to approach their work in a similar manner. If I embrace the struggle with interest and a positive attitude, my students are much more likely to follow my lead. Even if the material is hard. Even if it is quite laborious and time consuming. My attitude in the classroom makes a difference. As a teacher, I hold tremendous power over the daily experiences of my students. I take this very seriously.

### We Learn What We See

In my lifetime as a student, I have been incredibly lucky to have encountered passionate teachers at every turn. Some still stand out in my mind—and likely always will. They fully embraced and embodied this "*How* you teach is *What* you teach" philosophy in their classrooms. Certain people instantly come back to me as those whose passionate teaching styles mirrored their interest in their subject area. This was important.

To be quite honest, I didn't really need my English teachers to "sell" English to me—I already loved it. Their passion for characters, authors, writing, argument, and everything else that came with that class just enhanced my overall experience. But in subject areas where I was not as confident as a student, or even felt downright bored with the material, my teachers' attitude and passion for their content directly influenced my attitude and passion toward the material.

When I think of impassioned teaching, three teachers come to mind who significantly impacted me as a student: my American Literature teacher, my Algebra I teacher, and my Chemistry teacher. I remember these people not necessarily for individual content lessons, but for loving their content area—loving it so much that I thought to myself, "I guess this can't be too bad. I'll give it a shot." They delivered lessons with energy and sincere enthusiasm, and always expressed genuine concern for me and my educational experience.

My American Literature teacher was one of the most positive, reassuring people I encountered throughout my time in high school. Her enthusiasm for literature was palpable. When I spoke to her, it was clear that I had her complete attention, and she listened sincerely to each of us when we made contributions to discussions in her class. Her comments on my essays were encouraging while still challenging, and she would flit happily around the classroom speaking so sincerely of her love for each author we studied that I was convinced each writer was one of her personal best friends and confidants.

My Algebra I teacher would stand at the chalkboard, and, while demonstrating to the class how to work out a math problem, she would turn to us and say with a grin, "Isn't this fun?!" This was intriguing to me. Never before had I thought of math in any way other than as a chore to complete each night. I had never considered it something I would willingly *want* to do, and I certainly had never considered it fun. While I was making every effort to avoid being called on—painstakingly averting my eyes and sinking lower in my seat, all the while willing myself invisible—she was gleefully and swiftly working her way through problems. I was quite certain I'd die of embarrassment if I were called up to the board to do the same thing, and yet there she was, completely engrossed in her work, and genuinely enjoying it.

My Chemistry teacher's influence stands out most in my mind, though. When people ask me about my favorite high school teacher, I'm sure they assume I'll wax poetic about a former English or Music teacher (music was my other passion as a student). Instead, I break into excited chatter about my Chemistry teacher. She, too, embodied an excitement for her content that my sixteen-year-old self would never have thought possible. But she offered an even more complete experience in her classroom. Her love of both her content *and* her students, coupled with a variety of active teaching strategies, kept us engaged throughout each lesson. She knew the power of active learning and constant checking for understanding in order to support students who needed clarification, re-teaching, or extra support. And she did all this while teaching a difficult subject. She sincerely believed everyone could learn chemistry, and her engaging lessons and contagious enthusiasm caused me (the English/Music student) to believe this, too. In fact, she has been one of the biggest influences on me and the educator I am today.

In 2011, this teacher was nominated for an Educator of the Year award, and her department chair contacted me about writing her a letter of recommendation for this award. Here is a little of what I wrote about her:

> [My Chemistry teacher's] guidance and philosophy of education
> have greatly shaped me as an educator and as a person today....
> As an instructor, [she] went out of her way to ensure each student

understood the day's content. Her lessons were engaging and interesting in ways I never knew that science could be.... As a motivator, you'll find no replacement—[she] was always my biggest fan, and I'd argue that every single one of my peers felt the same way. As a role model, [she] taught us what it meant to love learning—she embodies the concept of learning and experiencing, not for the grade, but for the richness it brings to your life.... I still remember a story [she] told us about going to the fireworks with her husband. She said they'd bring special glasses to the show and watch the colors in the fireworks through the special lenses. Some thought this was a little "dorky," but I thought it was fantastic! She was a constant reminder that life is about learning and fully embracing the process. I often tell my English students during a heated debate or an animated discussion of writing or literature that "I revel in my nerdiness." It's true, I do. I learned to do that from others who weren't afraid to revel in theirs. In this regard, I have [her] to thank. She made it ok to love learning, she made it ok to talk about learning, she made it ok to come in early for extra help, and she made it ok to take pride in all of that.

My Chemistry teacher won the High School Educator of the Year award that year. And in my opinion, there was no one more deserving of that award in the room that night. Each of these three teachers has impacted me in ways that extend far beyond the English, Math, or Chemistry classroom. Many of the lessons I took from them about learning and about being an active participant in the learning process have traveled with me throughout my higher education, and are now present in my own classroom.

### In the End

One of the things that makes this job so simultaneously fulfilling and infuriating is the human component. David Labaree (2008) of Stanford University puts it like this:

Teaching is an extraordinarily difficult job that looks easy, which is a devastating combination for its professional standing and for the standing of its professional educators. Why is teaching so difficult?

One reason is that teaching cannot succeed without the compliance of the student. Most professions can carry out their work independent of the client; surgeons operate on the anesthetized and lawyers defend the mute. But, teachers can only accomplish their goals if students are willing to learn. They exert their efforts to motivate student compliance in the task of learning, but they cannot on their own make learning happen.

As teachers, part of our job is to help students channel this willingness and motivation to learn. Certainly, this inspiration comes from a number of places, but passion for our content and craft is a good place to start. We're never going to be able to save every student from circumstances over which we have no control, nor are we going to change the lives of all the students who walk into our classrooms. But we can work to make their day brighter, their learning clearer, their love for subjects deeper, and their resolve to continue trying each and every day stronger. We do this by tirelessly caring, supporting, nurturing, and challenging our students. In this endeavor, we model for our students a lifelong love of learning, and we empower motivated, conscientious citizens of the future.

Indeed, how we teach is what we teach.

## References

Banner, J.M., & Cannon, H.C. (1997). *The elements of teaching*. New Haven, CT: Yale University Press.

Eisner, E.W. (1991). *The enlightened eye*. New York: Macmillan.

Greene, M. (1967). *Existential encounters for teachers*. New York: Random House.

Greene, M. (1995). *Releasing the imagination: Essays on education, the arts, and social change*. San Francisco, CA: Jossey-Bass.

Labaree, D.F. (2008). An uneasy relationship: The history of teacher education in the university. In M. Cochran-Smith, S. Feiman Nemser, & D.J. McIntyre (Eds.), *Handbook of research on teacher education: Enduring issues in changing contexts* (3rd ed., pp. 290–306). Washington, DC: Association of Teacher Educators.

Noddings, N. (2003). *Happiness and education.* New York: Cambridge University Press.

Tricarico, D. (2015). *The zen teacher.* San Diego, CA: Dave Burgess Consulting, Inc.

Wong, H., & Wong, R. (1991). *The first days of school.* Mountainview, CA: Harry K. Wong Publications.

# CHAPTER TWO

# INVITATIONAL LEARNING
## Building School Culture *with Love*

BARBARA J. MALLORY AND JAMES DAVIS

IN AN ERA OF a marketplace of schools—from virtual schools and charter schools, to public schools and private—educators have a choice about where they want to teach. Although many studies have been conducted on why teachers want to teach, for purposes of this chapter we considered *where* teachers want to teach and students want to learn. While some teachers may seek to teach in a school with a strong principal, others may select a school known for integrating technology across the curriculum. While some students view their school as a "prison," others describe their school as a safe haven. Where is an ideal place to teach and learn? Where do teachers want to teach, principals want to lead, and students want to learn? Our assumption in this chapter is that teachers want to teach in a place where everyone, including students, "loves school."

Having served as principals, we know how important it is for students and teachers to love school and for families to love their child's school. Through the eyes of a principal, that often means the school has, or is intentionally building, an inviting school culture and climate. What is an invitational school culture that draws people in and causes them to care about their school? It is one that deliberately and purposefully seeks to engage students through a caring and inspiring environment, regardless of students' zip codes or unique characteristics. It is a culture that, rather than sorting and selecting students, and rather than catering to the best teachers, focuses on embracing the school as a community of learners. Who would not love a school where students view themselves not as prisoners stripped of their freedom but as individuals invited to learn with others in places that are inspiring and that are guided by policies, programs, and processes that encourage everyone to be fully engaged?

To build a school culture and climate that promotes a "love connection" among all within the school community, the people of, for, and by the school need to develop a vision of what this school looks like and then use resources within to build an inspiring environment with caring people. That is, to build a love connection, the people within must examine the vision of the ideal school culture through the lens of the current culture and climate of their school. Is this current school a place where teachers, staff, students, and their parents, or "extended family," feel a sense of belonging?

This sense of belonging is at the core of a love relationship with school (Stanley, Juhnke, & Purkey, 2004). This chapter explains how an "invitational" school and classroom culture and climate can inspire a student's high interest, engagement, and passion for learning. We provide examples from two schools to demonstrate what principals and teacher leaders may consider as they reflect on the question "Do students have a love connection with our school?" An "invitational" culture and school climate that focus on positive environments and result in "love" relationships, in contrast to a school culture and climate that demean and defeat human potential, resulting in "hate" relationships, is the central focus of this chapter.

First, however, let's consider why a caring environment in schools matters. Why is it important to consider the love connection of school culture and climate when thinking about teachers and the schools in which they are, or want to be, teaching? To answer that question, we have to go back to Rosenholtz (1991), who described the school as a social organization, asserting that "Teachers, like members of most organizations, shape their beliefs and actions largely in conformance with the structures, policies, and traditions of the workaday world around them" (pp. 2–3). Every school has a culture, defined broadly as "the way we do things around here," and every school has a climate, broadly defined as "the way we feel about the way we do things around here." Peterson and Deal (2002) explained: "Culture is a powerful web of rituals and traditions, norms and values that affect every corner of school life" (p. 10). The beliefs, symbols, stories, rites of passage,

and ceremonies that communicate to the world "who we are" are also powerful forces that determine how people identify with the school and how
committed they are to it.

Commitment to schools happens when students and families feel their
needs are being addressed. It happens especially when schools dedicate themselves to having a "student-centered focus" (Schoen & Teddlie, 2008). A
student-centered focus involves "assessing the extent to which needs of individual students are met by the school's programs, policies, rituals, routines,
and traditions" (p. 141). One way to assess whether the needs of individual
students are being met—and a central way in the current talk about teaching—
is to use student data to make instructional decisions in ways that contribute
to students' self-worth and self-efficacy. This practice can, if done correctly,
build a student's sense of self-direction, which in turn can drive his or her
commitment to school. This practice can build commitment to human growth
and development, which is at the heart of a love connection with school.

On a continuum, school climate can vary from, on the one end, close to
toxic, to, on the other end, what Barth (2001) describes as "an ethos hospitable to the promotion of human learning" (p. 11). Principals and teachers who aim for an ethos that promotes commitment to learning have the
potential to build a school that students love. However, in schools where
students are not encouraged to discuss their purpose for being in school,
and not encouraged to build their capacity to fulfill their purpose, climate
toxicity may prevail, thus lessening the likelihood that students will love
their school. An absence of student-centered practices communicates that
the school exists for other purposes rather than to help build capacity for
individual student growth and development. Schools may be the last institutions on earth that have the opportunity to bring all of the community
together around a common bond—that of promoting a purpose-driven
school that uses inquiry and a love of building everyone's capacity in an
inspiring environment.

### The 5 Ps of Invitational Culture

If we are intentional about building a healthy culture and climate to draw
students and their families in for the purpose of learning, let's delve deeper
into critical components of culture and climate that help build commitment
to school. As a learning and teaching organization, school is a social place.
Purkey (1993) described the social aspects of school culture and climate by

introducing the concept of "invitational education," using a starfish with its five arms to explain a framework for making schools caring, exciting, and dynamic for all students, faculty, and the various communities served by the school.

The depiction of starfish arms, with each representing one of the five P's of invitational learning, helps to visualize the components of culture and climate that matter in building schools where students might forge a "love connection." The five P's—people, places, policies, programs, and processes—must work in concert, just as a starfish needs all of its "arms" to navigate successfully in its world. Purkey and Novak (2008) chose the starfish as the metaphor for building an inviting school culture and climate because building the love connection is not just about people in the school. It is not just about physical spaces that are inviting; neither is it just policies that engage parents as meaningful partners in schools. It is not just about programs that link students to high engagement, nor is it just about processes that build capacity, connections, and the confidence of students, teachers, and parents. Rather, it is the sum total of all of the five P's that builds the type of school culture and climate that contribute to a student's liking school. Just as a starfish uses all its arms to gently massage an oyster that it wants to consume, the gentle pressure of all five P's working in concert in an intentional way contributes to an "inviting culture and climate" designed to help make teaching and learning a collaborative enterprise with students, teachers, staff, and parents.

It is interesting to note that there are no fiscal costs involved in building a school culture and climate where kids love school and become committed to it. In the schools we describe in this chapter, we emphasize that the intentional decision to build a caring culture and climate is *through* and *with* people *within* the school. The internal coherence they seek to build in reality is a network among the five P's. Education is a human enterprise; therefore, it always starts with "people." Barth (2006) makes this argument when he advises school leaders in these words: "Relationships among educators within a school range from vigorously healthy to dangerously competitive. Strengthen those relationships, and you improve professional practice" (p. 8).

## Hospitable School #1

Drawing from our experience as principals, we share here what we came to understand about schools that work to build invitational learning cultures.

We were principals in the two schools described below, which we call Hospitable School #1 (HS#1) and Hospitable School #2 (HS#2). As we reflect back on the principalships we enjoyed, we realize how intentional we were in building a school culture where everyone had an invitational learning mindset. By providing some examples of the five P's discussed above—people, places, policies, programs, and processes—we hope that readers may reflect on their own school culture through the lens of the starfish metaphor.

When I (Barbara Mallory) was principal at HS#1, it was a high school with approximately 1,400 students. The school was a majority-minority school—that is, most students attending (66%) were non-White, and most of these were African American. Approximately 16% of the students were Hispanic, 4% Asian, 34% White, and 10% denoted as "two or more races." The school is located within the city limits of an urban area with a population just above 110,000. By all indicators typically used to describe school success, the school was first-rate, with an 89% graduation rate, 100% highly qualified teachers, 98% attendance rate, and performance scores on state tests all "above the state average."

What was particularly noteworthy about the school, however, was that it also scored well on two surveys, one that measured teacher working conditions and another that measured student climate. In reflecting on why the school was rated so highly in working conditions and student climate, I wanted to capture "an answer," even as I knew it involved the dynamics and interactions of many factors related to our people, our school building and location, our student-centered policies, our abundance of programs and events to engage students, and our processes, which seemed to stay in continuous improvement mode. The HS#1 school culture was very student- and teacher-centered, with many opportunities to communicate and engage with families and community members. What follows is a snapshot of the invitational learning culture as experienced through the five P's—people, places, policies, programs, and processes.

**The people.** First, in HS#1, the "people" were important, as evidenced by the level of engagement of teachers, students, and parents. The people within the school who were most directly critical to student success, including the principal, teachers, students, staff, and families, all shared a "love condition" within the school culture. The people within the school were truly committed to the work of teaching and learning and development of human capacity. If anyone were to walk the halls and listen to conversations, he or she would hear laughter, exchanges about teaching practices, or "the next" learning opportunity. Intercom announcements and the student live-streaming messages extolled the successes of students and celebrated teach-able moments. Teachers stood at their classroom doors greeting students with personalized messages, such as "loved that catch you made last night," or just a fist bump for each student.

As a principal, I never wanted to direct the choices teachers made in their professional learning. I always encouraged professional growth, but my leadership involved asking teachers about their needs and opportunities for growth. Professional learning communities (PLCs) operated organically, based on need and a clear and shared focus, and teachers were not made to participate in a PLC. Talking to teachers in the school, one would get the impression that the faculty were compelled to live the mission of "achieve-ment abounds," but the choices about how to do that varied by individual and by department. In the math department, teachers often met in groups to plan what's next for a group of struggling students or to share why they believe an innovative practice is working with another group of students. In the career and technical department, however, teachers met more frequently in groups to address operational issues (such as budgets) that are aligned with "experiential learning."

In walking the halls of HS#1, one could also observe students with high expectations of their engagement. They were laughing and talking between classes, but when bells would ring, everyone was in class. Routines and protocols were evident as students logged into a lesson or set up their sci-ence lab. In HS#1, one example of engagement was "the senior project." All seniors undertook a senior project that spanned the entire year, and it involved each senior's connection with a community mentor. The senior had an advisor who met and planned with him or her in selecting a topic that was relevant, meaningful, and interesting to that student. The project had to be related to personal growth, with a link to how it could benefit the community. Each and every senior presented his or her project to a panel of school and community members. One would see not just seniors from honors classes or a select group taking part, but participation of *all* seniors, which provided a bonding activity for a meaningful senior-year experience. I still receive messages from seniors who graduated 15 years ago about how meaningful the experience was, especially in terms of the relationships that were an outgrowth of it.

Parents, including a JROTC Advisory group, had a critical voice in the activities of the school. Imagine a school with so many booster groups—from band boosters and sports boosters to orchestra boosters and STEM boosters—that they also created one overarching Parent Academic Advisory group to coordinate dates, events, and activities. Not just Academic Boosters, but all booster groups had a clear and focused mission "linked to learning." One indication of high levels of communication and collaboration among parents is that one parent coordinated transportation opportunities for parents who might not have a car or other means by which to attend events. No one was forgotten, left behind, or not engaged by choice.

**The place.** The second "P," the place of school culture, focuses on the school facility, which in the case of HS#1 was a building constructed in the 1970s. The greenhouse provided a good example of how "place" in an inviting school culture works. The greenhouse was located near the front of the school, and it operated as a laboratory for both botany and horticulture classes. Students in science classes studied structure, genetics, ecology, and classification of plants in partnership with students in horticulture. The career and technical-education students in horticulture applied knowledge of how plants grow directly to the care and utilization of plants in different landscapes throughout the school. They sold plants to the public, which provided a connection of "school" to "community."

The place called school also provided a supportive learning environment that engaged all students who co-created and designed projects, many of which later decorated the school. Student artwork was always visible in the halls, as well as "growth charts" from physical education classes. The physical space appeared inviting, with posters, banners, and slogans all appearing as though they were just put up the day before to showcase what was happening or about to happen in HS#1. The school provided good signage for volunteers who came into the school every day, as the halls were long and the school very spread out. (It was a one-story facility that served almost 2,000 people daily.)

Another aspect of "place" that demonstrated an "inviting culture" was the Morning Café run by students with special needs. Students chatted with peers as they filled orders for biscuits or fruit, and they provided change to teachers who ordered their morning blend. The pocket change was often left in a "car jar" at the counter. The change was used to support "transportation" needs of parents to attend IEP meetings or athletic events. It took much effort to create such a space, as health department regulations and food service codes had to be observed, but in a school that wants to draw students in, one way is to create high levels of engagement. Students in food services classes can be very engaged in helping to navigate the complexities of opening a café within a school.

**The policies.** The third "P" of invitational learning school culture is "policies." Local schools are subject to state and school district policies, but those policies can sometimes be adapted to fit the local school's people and vision of school culture. For example, in HS#1, the district Code of Conduct outlined "suspendable offenses," in which the principal had some input in decisions that "may result in suspension." Together with students, parents, and teachers, HS#1 designed a Saturday School for first offenders, thus providing an option other than suspension for students who violated the school district's Code of Conduct. They used an approach of equity and fairness in designing school policies to prevent students from seeing school as a "place where they were mistreated." Policies reflected practices about good citizenship—always with teaching and learning in mind.

**The programs.** The fourth "P," the "programs" of an inviting school culture, were also evident in HS#1, where a large majority of students (90%) reported in the "School Culture Survey" that "Students at my school support most extra-curricular activities (not just sports)." The school had a vast menu of "extra-curricular and co-curricular" programs and was open from 7:00 A.M. until 9:00 P.M., six days a week (and sometimes seven, when theater rehearsals were in full swing). The majority of programs were "linked to learning," a characteristic of this inviting school culture.

**The processes.** Finally, the fifth "P," the processes within the school, were observed through means by which policies were enacted. The doors, although often locked just as a safety precaution, were very inviting to guests and visitors, with signs and quick service to welcome visitors and guests in a friendly manner. The telephones were always answered with a welcoming message: "Thank you for calling HS#1." When I was principal, a neighboring principal in the school district used this message: "Thank you for calling our school, where learning abounds. How may we assist you?" There were many classroom routines that helped students know and follow expectations, and there were many student routines, such as homecoming rituals and traditions, that resulted in high levels of engagement. Another indicator of the invitational culture was the number of alumni who came back, not just during homecoming season, but for sporting and cultural arts events. When they did return, they regularly shared at least one experience from their days at HS#1, which demonstrated their love for the school.

Another process that demonstrated student-centeredness was the operation of an "honor council" run for and by students. The students operated the council during lunch as a "peer court" in which students could choose to attend to discuss a first-time, Category 1 discipline infraction, rather than being disciplined by an assistant principal. The peer honor council shared outcomes of the proceedings with the assistant principal. The signature characteristic of HS#1's processes was clear communication for, of, and by the people.

Thanks to the inviting school culture, students seemed to like their school. In response to the item "I feel that I belong (am accepted and liked) at school" on school culture surveys, 93% answered "strongly agree." This school thrived in an invitational learning culture, making it a place where teachers wanted to teach and students wanted to learn. The culture of HS#1 attracted students and teachers. Students, teachers, and families all felt a strong sense of belonging, the hallmark of an invitational learning culture. A retired teacher group meets annually, bonded by a sense of commitment to a school where they played an integral part in building a loving culture.

## Hospitable School #2

The next journey leads us to an elementary school, one that fully embraced the Purkey concepts and all five P's. When I (James Davis) was principal of HS#2, an elementary school, we had a student population of approximately 1,000, grades pre-K to 5. HS#2 was roughly half White and half non-White, with a free and reduced lunch rate of 80%. The school and all stakeholders had been recognized for high levels of academic growth over a two-year period, but chronically struggled with high levels of proficiency. Our students demonstrated high levels of growth each year, and I was always proud when HS#2 was showcased in the state for innovative learning practices, high student attendance, high teacher attendance, and "greater than normal" gains in reading, math, and science.

HS#2 is located amid both suburban and urban-esque populations. The campus is home to students from traditional families, non-traditional families, subsidized housing, and orphanages, as well as homeless students. This school, like others in the area, had teachers who were highly qualified, with more than one-third of them holding advanced degrees. There were roughly six to seven classrooms per grade level K–5, with a principal, two assistant principals, and two lead teachers, one specializing in math and science and one with an area of expertise built around reading and writing. From one end of campus to the other, the five P's were prevalent.

**The people.** Beginning with "people," so much can be encompassed with a meaningful mission statement prominently displayed in the school's entrance. Priorities were obvious to visitors walking into HS#2, and people were front and center. Imagine a professional banner, mounted for all to see, outlining the school's mission to "Love Kids, Support Teachers, Involve Parents, and Pass It On!" On the first day of school and throughout the year, one could hear students, teachers, and parents discussing each component of the mission statement, built around "people."

At HS#2, administrators regularly met to discuss what it means to "love kids." As principal of the school, I often heard dialogue about teaching well every day for the "love of our kids." When students were hungry, we found ways to feed them. When a child needed to talk, we had caring adults— either counselors, or teachers, or administrators—who listened. We offered pencil and paper as needed. Loving them always meant teaching them well every day at HS#2.

Teachers in HS#2 engaged in collaborative activities. Grade-level meetings focused on what support teachers needed to help students. Strong collaboration also took place between teachers and families in the teacher workroom, where PTO members often met during the school day, alongside faculty. One major PTO commitment was to recognize and celebrate any and all kinds of family engagement with the school. Family engagement did not just mean a "parent volunteer." The PTO recognized all manner of activities that families and their children engaged in to support the school and the child's learning.

We also continued to expand the school's mission by engaging community members in discussions about how to "pass it on." At HS#2, many amazing things happened. Some people were spotlighted, and other individuals began to inquire about some of the significant learning and events taking place on our campus. With a mission statement that the school believed in and used as a daily roadmap for changing lives, the message was shared loud and clear in our school: *all* people matter here. Living the mission in any school helps build school commitment that manifests itself in love for one's school, not hate.

**The place.** One of the key places in HS#2 was the "think tank"—a conference room specifically linked to the purpose of our work together. In that room the focus was on keeping the "main" thing just that: the "main" thing. HS#2's "think tank" set a tone and served a purpose. The "think tank" was a comfortable area with resources available, where groups of stakeholders could come together to strengthen a school family, push the bar upward, and create action steps toward reaching goals associated with sustainability and new initiatives.

On any given day in the "think tank," a visitor to our school may have found students creating a plan of action for a service learning project, or parents hosting a focus group, or teachers sharing inventive practices, or administrators brainstorming solutions to a current problem, or community stakeholders developing multi-tiered systems of support for people in the school. In the end, this "place" sent the message that everyone had something meaningful to contribute to building HS#2 as a place where learning and growth for all mattered. The "think tank" generated ideas, plans for implementation, and blueprints for higher levels of teaching and learning. It was a key reason why we were all glad to be teaching and helping at our school.

**The policies.** As principal, I realized there were a couple of bottom-line statements when it came to the merging of policies in an invitational school. We recognized these statements as truth:

- Some policies are within our control as building-level leaders.

- Some policies are not within our control as building-level leaders.

With that said, we reduced complaints regarding policies and focused on actions to assimilate and communicate policies. Not being able to control all policies did not hinder us from impacting policy implementation in a student-centered, progressive, positive way. As principal of HS#2, I explained a district policy as it related to students and school-level discipline practices. "It is our district policy to discipline students via a 3-step process from which we will not deviate. Those 3 steps will include punitive actions, educational sanctions, and a mandatory clean-slate statement." In great detail, I explained the following:

- **Positive Component:** At times, it is appropriate to give a student a punitive consequence for an action he or she engaged in while at school.

When a punitive consequence is required, it will be directly linked to the misbehavior, and a conversation will be had with the student explaining the real purpose of the consequence—that is, it is designed to minimize the misbehavior and therefore lead to greater levels of student success.

- **Educational Component:** With each disciplinary incident, there is a required educational component. When a punitive component is delivered, it is immediately followed by a required teachable moment. The required educational component may begin with something such as:

  - What could you do differently next time?
  - Who could you have sought out for help?
  - Here are some suggestions I have if you are in this situation again.

- **Clean-Slate Component:** Finally, there is a clean-slate component. If a child misbehaves, he or she may receive a punitive consequence, engage in an educational/teachable moment, and then transition into the clean-slate statement. The clean-slate statement may begin with something such as: "Everyone messes up. As long as we learn from our mistakes, that is the most important thing. Today you broke a rule. I provided you with a consequence, not to be mean, but to help you refrain from repeating this behavior in the future. I want you to be successful, and we talked about some better choices that you could make if you are ever in this situation again. Finally, tomorrow is a new day. You come back to my class with a clean slate. I will only bring this misbehavior up again if you initiate the conversation or I see the behavior repeated. Otherwise, live and learn."

While all disciplinary offenses did not fit into categorized boxes, the premise was clear to our families, students, and faculty: all of HS#2's policies will be structured and implemented in a manner in which each student in this school is learning, growing, and feeling as though he or she belongs, and will be held accountable for good citizenship on our campus. Student commitment to school, even when punitive actions were warranted, did not have to be lost if, through communication, caring adults handled situations as teaching and learning moments in time.

**The programs.** With an invitational school culture and climate at the forefront of everyone's minds, it is important to recognize that programs can be differentiated to meet individual needs. As principal, I viewed how program offerings could be experienced through the eyes of students, teachers, and parents. In every program, from extracurricular activities to parent workshops, differentiation was key. One size did not fit all when it came to implementing programs.

As an example, at HS#2, the administrative team often discussed how we lived our mission: "Love Kids, Support Teachers, Involve Parents, and Pass It On!" In our "support" program for teachers, we recognized that we needed to provide support in a differentiated way, as the concept of "support" is relevant to the individual needs of teachers. In our teacher support program, we identified whole-group and individual types of support. For example, to demonstrate support for beginning teachers, we showcased beginning teachers in a multitude of ways. They could shine, even in their first year!

Since all teachers often expressed the need for "more time" as a way to support them, we developed a variety of ways to make that time available. Using coupons, we targeted paths to "free time" for teachers to support them in the many tasks required in teaching. Imagine the look on a new teacher's face when he received a digital coupon from the administrative team, offering to assess up to 150 student assignments to be scored by the administrative team in the next grading period. A veteran teacher may have received a coupon with an administrator offering "to teach for a day" in his or her classroom, freeing up time to engage in mentoring activities. The simple fact that school leaders extended these various "support" tactics communicated the message: "You matter; I am here for you; and I am willing to serve you." In an invitational school with the mission "Love Kids, Support Teachers, Involve Parents, and Pass It On!," diverse support strategies that denoted a caring environment were designed to increase commitment to the school, thus distinguishing it as a place where teachers wanted to teach.

**The processes.** Processes matter when it comes to achieving various kinds of results associated with an invitational school culture and climate. HS#2 had a multitude of processes for virtually every task. As principal, it was a high priority for me that tasks were spelled out and shared in a clear manner. Processes were not about control, but rather about valuing stakeholders, planning with a purpose, and treating everyone in a manner that says, "You belong."

At our school, one of the key processes we used was data team meetings. A data team meeting is one in which assigned team members may collect, review, and analyze data for the sake of growth as it relates to student achievement. I clarified how this would be different in our school. While we used the same basic definition, we added a component. At HS#2, every member of our data team was assigned a special population to advocate for during all meetings (academic, attendance, discipline, etc.). Regardless of the topic, someone was to advocate for everyone. Our intention was to build processes that showcase that our people matter and that, in the end, our goal was that no child falls through the cracks.

Professional development was another key process for us. Professional development efforts are targeted/planned action steps that are taken to strengthen teachers and make them better prepared to do their jobs successfully on a daily basis. Again, while we used the same basic definition for professional development in our school, we also had a process in which educators had a greater voice. With our professional development process, teachers could often choose items such as the time (morning, afternoon), place (classroom, media center), topic (to some degree), presenters (administrators, fellow teachers), and format (online, face-to-face) of the professional development. A greater voice leads to increased accountability and, therefore, an increase in results.

Processes say to all involved, "I cared enough to plan ahead, and I cared enough to incorporate you and your voice into our efforts."

## The Inverse of Hospitable Schools

The inverse of an invitational culture, such as the cultures identified in HS#1 and HS#2, can be observed by walking through schoolhouse doors. If people are unenthusiastic, not smiling, participating in PLCs because of coercion, engaging in whole-group professional learning activities that seem focused on "one and done" rather than "collaborate to elaborate," *those might be danger signs of an uninviting school culture*. It is difficult to build commitment in toxic cultures, a deficiency that leads to "school hate." If the place has no student work visible or if teachers are not welcoming students to class, *that might be a danger sign of an uninviting school culture*. If school policies and rules are visible everywhere, and the school appears to communicate policies warning students of consequences rather than encouraging them to be good citizens, *that might be a danger sign of an uninviting school culture*. If an observer sees examples of programs that direct students, rather than encouraging self-direction about participating, or one sees programs that are offered that tend to sort and select students (you have to be on the honor roll to be a member of this club) rather than inviting students to network and learn with and from each other, *that might be a danger sign of an uninviting school culture.* If school competitions and celebrations are about the "best" rather than about "collaboration to celebration" and "competition to learn from each other," *that might be a danger sign of an uninviting school culture.* If administrators and teachers do not model the school's mission through visible behaviors every single day, the school is in danger of building a toxic culture that produces students and teachers who hate the school. An invitational culture, by contrast, offers the possibility for teachers and students to love their schools.

## School Culture Matters

Is it possible to build an invitational culture where students have a "love connection" at school? It is possible through intentional planning and monitoring of the school culture that focuses on the degree to which that culture and climate are inviting. Culture matters! If principals and teachers want an invitational learning culture in which all five P's are operating at a high level of involvement, with extraordinary expectations of student success through a caring and supporting environment, it can happen. If the school climate emanates positivity, then students and teachers tend to "fall in love" with school (Freiberg, 1999). Freiberg (1999) described school climate as the heart and soul of the school and the essence of the school that draws teachers and students to love the school and to want to be part of it. Students feel valued and thrive in an environment where positive emotions of teachers are present (Cobb, 2014).

It all starts with crucial conversations among those within the school. These conversations begin with essential questions through which rich and honest discussion can form the basis for meaningful action. Regarding people, the school staff can determine the level of interdependence of people. What is "interdependence" in our school? What strategies do we use, and what practices do we promote to engage students and build interdependence of parents, students, teachers, and staff? What evidence do we have from teachers, students, and parents that can provide a baseline of our cultural health and our inviting environment? What are places, policies, programs, and processes that our "people" believe we need to examine because they alienate students, teachers, or parents?

Although we might choose to teach in a school with an "invitational culture," we also would choose to teach in a school that wanted *to build* an invitational culture. Although many surveys are conducted to help establish the "health" of invitational culture, we suggest collecting data from teachers, students, and families using the kind of elements identified in what follows. These are sample survey items that would be presented to students, teachers, and parents. We would suggest using a Likert scale that gives respondents an opportunity to "strongly disagree," "disagree," "somewhat agree," or "strongly agree" to each item. Here are the items we suggest be included:

- Students have respect for other students
- Students have respect for teachers
- Teachers have respect for other teachers
- Teachers have respect for students
- School is a safe place inside the classroom
- School is a safe place outside the classroom
- School appears to be a place where everyone has pride and ownership
- Policies are fair
- Faculty and staff value what students have to say
- Students are involved in decisions that impact them in school
- Teachers are involved in decisions that impact them in school
- Families are involved in school decisions that impact them
- School has programs that build a cooperative spirit
- School has programs for everyone
- School has programs that demonstrate respect for people of all races and cultures
- Students in my school care about learning
- Teachers in my school care about learning
- Teachers are enthusiastic about teaching
- School's processes demonstrate that people are most important
- School disciplines students fairly
- School has classes that are enjoyable yet challenging
- In general, I like this school
- In general, I dislike this school

And, then, at the end: a prompt that invites people to pick three things they would do to improve the school. They could pick things having to do with people, the place, policies, programs, or processes.

If we, as educators, are committed to building school as a place where students like school rather than suffer through it, then we pay attention to classroom culture and climate, and we work daily to have our school culture and climate described in an honest manner as "inviting" and "caring." Although Purkey's (1993) theory of invitational learning involves many factors in addition to the five P's, in this chapter we have focused on describing an "invitational culture and climate" that draws students in, rather than pushing them out. With shifting demographics in schools and diversity in many classrooms, Schmidt (2004) explained how invitational learning principles can be helpful in working with issues of diversity. Everyone has a role in building school culture related to the five P's, with potential to build capacity for a love connection. As John Maxwell states: "Leadership is not about titles, positions or flowcharts. It is about one life influencing another" (qtd. in Walter, 2013). Authentic educators always have the desire and ability within their hearts to influence a student's love connection to school.

## References

Barth, R. (2001). *Learning by heart*. San Francisco, CA: Jossey-Bass.

Barth, R. (2006). Improving relationships within the schoolhouse. *Educational Leadership*, 63(6), 8–13.

Cobb, N. (2014). Climate, culture and collaboration: The key to creating safe and supportive schools. *Techniques: Connecting Education & Careers*, 89(7), 14–19.

Freiberg, H. (1999). School climate: Measuring, improving and sustaining healthy learning environments. London: Falmer Press.

Peterson, K.D., & Deal, T.E. (2002). *The shaping school culture fieldbook*. San Francisco, CA: Jossey-Bass.

Purkey, W.W. (1993). An introduction to invitational theory. *Journal of Invitational Theory and Practice*, 1(1), 5–15.

Purkey, W.W., & Novak, J. (2008). *Fundamentals of invitational education*. Kennesaw, GA: International Alliance for Invitational Education.

Rosenholtz, S.J. (1991). *Teacher's workplace: The social organization of schools*. New York: Teachers College Press.

Schmidt, J.J. (2004). Diversity and invitational theory and practice. *Journal of Invitational Theory and Practice, 10*, 27–46.

Schoen, L.T., & Teddlie, C. (2008). A new model of school culture: A response to a call for conceptual clarity. *School Effectiveness and School Improvement, 19*(2), 129–153.

Stanley, P.H., Juhnke, G.A., & Purkey, W.W. (2004). Using an invitational theory of practice to create safe and successful schools. *Journal of Counseling & Development, 82*(3), 302–309.

Walter, E. (2013, September). 50 heavyweight leadership quotes. *Forbes.* Retrieved from https://www.forbes.com/sites/ekaterinawalter/2013/09/30/50-heavyweight-leadership-quotes/#282546732259

# CHAPTER THREE

# BEYOND CURRICULUM

## Students Don't Love School When Schools Don't Love Them Back

BARBARA J. ROSE

### Context

*"I am so sorry for what school is going to do to you."*

AT A PARTY AT my home, with the last days of summer waning and the peaceful view of lawn and lake all around, the incongruous words voiced an unknown future. My colleague was speaking to my six-day-old granddaughter. Seated, he held her, his head bowed toward her, whispering. The long arms on his six-foot, six-inch body sheltered the 22-inch-long newborn with a sense of earnestness and sadness.

My granddaughter is now 18 months old. Her learning is transparent and physical. When she hears new words, she stops what she is doing, looks intently at the speaker for tone, studies the position and movements of the mouth, and voices the word, carefully and slowly. When something sparks her curiosity, she studies through observation and touch. Her eyes and body signal concentration and intentionality with spirit and fierceness. Sometimes, when she is extremely focused, her tongue extends slightly from her mouth, a family trait shared by generations. Like other children her age, she is an eager and insatiable learner. She is in the care of those who love her—those who are invested in her success, her happiness, and her future. In a few short years, the bubble of protection will be pierced, and the world of school will be upon her. Will she be sheltered and embraced as she was by my colleague and her family? Will school lift or crush her spirit and identity? Will school, which she will likely enter with enthusiasm and love, love her back? What will school do to her?

For many students, "what school did to them" is remembered fondly. As a teacher educator, the majority of my college students "fit" in their K–12 educational experiences. They were rewarded for turning homework in on time, having involved parents, achieving on standardized tests, and compliance. Their "success" was measured by criteria that were neither reachable by all nor reflective of educational practices that allow all students to thrive. School did not "do to them" what it did for many of their peers, whose sense of failure was as sharply defined by educational practices as my students' sense of confidence and success.

Maya Angelou said, "I've learned that people will forget what you said, people will forget what you did, but people will never forget how you made them feel." In K–12 schools and teacher education programs, there is focus on content and skills, paralleling Angelou's "what you said" and "what you did." Too often, there is little emphasis on "how you made them feel."

My colleague was apologizing to my granddaughter because school, at best, will enhance her beliefs about herself and her abilities, but she will not know the ways in which school has limited her. At worst, she will be scarred by experiences that create a lifetime of self-doubt and insecurity about education. Her fragile and vulnerable position is shared by other children. Creating educational environments where *all* children can learn without enduring emotional harm is complex, but essential. The stakes are high.

This chapter will draw on personal experiences, my experiences as a teacher educator, and voices from the literature to explore these five questions: Why is how students feel about school important? What kinds of examples of policies and practices in school culture benefit some students and not others? How are those who "love school" also educationally disadvantaged and impacted by policies and practices that adversely impact those who "hate school"? Why do students' feelings about school remain unexamined in many schools and teacher education programs? What are strategies to dismantle barriers to "loving school"?

## Why Is How Students Feel about School Important?

*"And how are the children? All the children are well."*

In her recent book on educating African-American students, Boutte (2016) spotlights the example of the standard greeting among the Masai people of Kenya, which is "And how are the children?" and is followed by the traditional response (even for people without children of their own), "All the children are well." She notes the importance of valuing children in the culture, saying that "when the priorities of protecting the young and the powerless are in place, peace and safety prevail" (p. 2). "Protecting the young and the powerless" from harm, including the emotional harm that can be inflicted in schools, contributes to the success of educating children that is critical to society.

### Impact of Academic and Societal Success

How students feel about school is an important predictor of the success Boutte describes. Students will be more likely to succeed in schools academically when they feel schools "love them back." Teacher Aileen Moffitt describes the link by saying, "The children I teach are more likely to be productive members of society if they have a strong sense of self to accompany their mastery of the curriculum" (Scruggs, 2009). Her statement is at the core of why it is important for students to love school (or at least not hate school); for most students, the valuing of student identity by educators is a prerequisite to success in academics and in life.

I see the positive impact of being loved in the stories of my college students who thrived in school. Many talk about how a teacher inspired and supported them, and were instrumental in their decision to become teachers. The narrative is often something like this: "I have wanted to be a teacher since 3rd grade, when I had Mrs. X, who was the greatest teacher ever. I want to be a teacher and be just like her." When pressed about what exactly Mrs. X did and what it means to be "just like her," students struggle to articulate specifics, but it is always about—in the message of Maya Angelou—"how the teacher made them feel." It is not about how inspirational a lesson plan was, or even the teacher's content mastery of a subject. It is about relationships.

Most students will be impacted at some point by experiences that affect their perceptions of school or their own abilities. Most teachers are caring and respectful of their students' emotional well-being. But over the course of a child's life in schools, the chances of one or more assaults on the spirit—intended or unintended—are high. The following are areas of impact that occur.

## Pushing Students out of School

A child might respond to an assault on his or her spirit by leaving school prior to graduation. Students who leave school generally have had numerous negative experiences in schools, frequently beginning in early childhood. Approximately 1.2 million students leave school each year (League of Education Voters Foundation, 2011), a shocking number that reflects the impact of school on children and youth.

Another correlate to leaving school is that students in poverty and students of color are more likely to be suspended, expelled, arrested, or put into the criminal justice system for minor infractions than their White counterparts, instead of being given counseling or detention (NAACP Legal Defense Fund, 2017). The trend toward severe disciplinary practices in schools that model criminalization and liken practices in schools to those in prisons is called the "school-to-prison pipeline." (See Heitzeg, 2016, for a sociological overview of the school-to-prison pipeline, and Laura, 2014, for a personal account of the educational experience of her brother and its family-wide impact.)

The long history of using the term "dropout" for students who leave school before graduation illustrates the lack of responsibility taken by schools in graduation rates. "Dropout" implies student choice or failure, suggesting that students leave school because they are unmotivated or unable to achieve academically. The term "pushout," which is increasingly being used in professional literature (see Dignity in Schools, 2017), considers the role of forces external to the student, particularly as related to racial and socioeconomic bias, inequitable student discipline policies, emphasis on standardized testing and graduation examinations, and other factors. The difference in the language (student-deficit versus system-deficit) is important.

## Impact on Self-Esteem

I have encountered many college students who were academically successful in school and who did not suffer the extreme consequences of being pushed out, but were still affected by treatment in school. In one case, a first-year college student disclosed that he had not asked a question in class since 3rd grade, where he was publicly shamed by his teacher for "asking too many questions." What may have been intended as a casual comment by a teacher in the singular event had a long-term impact on the student. How did his unasked (and unanswered) questions impact his learning over the decade since his shaming? How long would his self-silencing have continued if he had not disclosed in my class what had happened? It took support from me and his peers throughout the semester to have him feel "safe" to ask questions again.

Students care deeply about what their teachers think about them, and teachers must therefore be vigilant about what they say and do. Some of the most painful stories that students share from their own experiences are instances in which they felt they disappointed their teachers. For example, two of my students recently described similar stories from early elementary school where their teachers used behavior charts as part of classroom discipline. In each case, the students' cards were moved from "green" ("good" behavior) to "yellow" ("problem" behavior). As six-year-olds, they were humiliated and felt that they were "bad," but also felt shame in letting down their teachers. Even now, as adults looking back at what happened, they easily recount the details and feelings of confusion and degradation that remain.

Each of my students told of an isolated incident that happened on one school day during one academic year. Often, children in classrooms are routinely labeled as "bad" on an ongoing basis. What is it like to be a six-year-old, sitting in a classroom every day, looking at the yellow or red card next to his or her name? Why are emotionally harmful practices such as behavior charts not banned in schools?

## Impact of Stigmatization of Neighborhoods and Communities

The stigmatization of schools based on the race and/or socio-economic demographics of the community also affects students. I have noticed a pattern among my own students in linking the status of their schools with their own abilities. For example, students who perceive that they are from "good" schools (e.g., affluent suburban schools, private schools, or predominantly White schools) feel that they are well-equipped for life and the college experience. Conversely, students who perceive that they are from "bad" schools (e.g., urban schools, schools of low socio-economic status, or schools wherein students of color predominate) are more likely to feel that they have educational deficiencies that will adversely impact their college experience. In both scenarios, I have observed that students sometimes conflate (often erroneously) their own abilities with their perceptions of the quality of their schools.

Is how students feel about school important to their success and lives? Unequivocally, yes. *So, how are the children? All the children are NOT well.*

## What Kinds of Policies and Practices in School Culture Benefit Some Students and Not Others?

*Did you hear about the rose that grew*
*from a crack in the concrete?*
*Proving nature's law is wrong it*
*learned to walk without having feet.*
*Funny it seems, but by keeping its dreams,*
*it learned to breathe fresh air.*
*Long live the rose that grew from concrete*
*when no one else ever cared.*

—Tupac Shakur (2000)

Policies and practices that benefit some students and not others flood schools, penetrating classrooms and school-family relationships. Shakur's poem highlights the externally driven challenges of privilege and deficit thinking that are encountered, and the resilience and tenacity of people to overcome those challenges. (See Gorski, 2011, for a discussion of deficit thinking.) The metaphor of the rose growing in concrete has been applied to education by Duncan-Andrade (2009, 2011), who describes his experience as a teacher in Oakland, California. In an application to curriculum, Kirkland (2008) explores the relationship of culturally relevant pedagogy to student learning in English education.

In this chapter, the concrete represents the seemingly impenetrable array of school policies and practices found in schools. Dense and solid, they are inflexible. The opaqueness and lack of transparency make critical questioning and deep examination of impact difficult. As noted in the previous section, examples can be found "early and often" in a child's educational experience, and impact is serious.

Although complex and difficult, the analysis of what creates the "concrete" in schools is the responsibility of educators, administrators, and teacher educators. As anyone who has ever written or drawn something in wet concrete knows, when initially poured, concrete can be shaped or altered. Once hardened, there is permanence of what is there, and reforming is difficult. So it is with many classroom practices and policies. What is hardened through repetition or tradition is often difficult to undo.

Every piece of the concrete that is education is fair game for analysis, and, just as important, *should* be studied, whether it is obvious (e.g., persistent bias, deficit thinking, shaming, or racism) or subtle (e.g., rigidity, compliance, unexamined practices, or self-reflection). A few examples from the latter category are included here to illustrate the relationship between the stories of education and their meaning.

### A Panorama from Three Scenes, One Child

From my perspective as a parent, I vividly remember the first (but not last) alarm bells that sounded in my daughter Brenna's formal education. My panoramic view was developed through three "scenes"—experiences in pre-kindergarten, 1st, and 2nd grades. Collectively, the three scenes provide a glimpse into the impact of teacher and administrator behaviors, curriculum, and school-family relationships.

Scene 1: When Brenna attended pre-kindergarten, she had two different teachers—one in the morning and one in the afternoon. The morning teacher was trained and licensed as a middle school teacher, the afternoon teacher in early childhood education. There was a dramatic difference in expectations for classroom behavior and academic achievement. The middle school teacher lacked understanding of what was developmentally appropriate for a four-year-old and frequently communicated studied deficiencies to students and families. Brenna loved both teachers. In her four-year-old mind, the teachers were, after all, her *teachers*—revered as an important part of this sacred space called school. Her loyalty was clear and poignant, but I observed her different behaviors in the two classrooms. In the morning, she worked intently to prove her worthiness and focused on doing what her teacher wanted. In the afternoon, she was relaxed, curious, and happy. "School didn't love her back" because a well-meaning teacher was not properly prepared, and an administrative system allowed that teacher to teach in ways that were not in the best interests of students.

**Scene 2:** Brenna prides herself on punctuality, a trait that began early and continues to this day. She was the child who begged me to take her to everything insanely early, with enough time to spare to change a flat tire or be delayed by unexpected traffic. One day in 1st grade, she arrived to school early, as usual, and was in the classroom. She was putting her backpack on the hook when the bell rang, and she was informed by her teacher that she would be counted as "late" since she wasn't seated at her desk. Brenna was inconsolable. The teacher, who knew full well Brenna's feelings about punctuality, stood firm. "The rule is...." was her response and defense. "School didn't love back that day" was imbedded in a rule that defied logic, a teacher whose rigidity would deeply distress a child, and the disconnect between crime and punishment.

**Scene 3:** When Brenna was in 2nd grade, I attended a parent-teacher conference where the teacher's sole agenda was to report scores from standardized tests. She shared the results with a "canned speech" tone, rattling off numbers without context and saying that the tests were designed to improve student performance. When I asked about what the numbers meant and how they would be used, she couldn't explain, saying that the teachers weren't trained to know and didn't use the test results at all anyway. She was clearly irritated with my questions and suggested I talk to the principal if I wanted more information. That moment confirmed that the externally created and mandated tests were not intended to help teachers or families, but were simply for aggregate reporting on school "report cards." When I met with the principal, she couldn't explain what the results meant and how they could be used either. She briefly looked at the scores, scanning for the lowest, and offered this chilling comment: "In my experience, girls just don't do as well in math as boys." My concern as a parent at that moment broadened well beyond scores or their meaning. School didn't "love my child back" because of gender bias, dismissiveness, and lack of professional knowledge.

I learned in my daughter's early experiences with school that what she learned in a classroom was not as important to me as how she felt about learning and about herself. Her preschool and kindergarten experiences, which I have not detailed here, were wonderful, with caring teachers who knew she was not "an empty vessel to be filled"—a frequently used metaphor in education, coined by Freire (1970)—but someone's *baby*. My learning is echoed in the work and lens of many scholars (e.g., Delpit, 2006; Ladson-Billings, 2009), who explore the ways that school cultures and curricula impact children.

### Two Pieces of Concrete Shattered by One Teacher, One Letter

In advance of the 2016–17 academic year, 2nd-grade teacher Brandy Young sent a letter to parents (Earl, 2016; see below) that went viral on social media and was widely reported in national news sources. The focus of most of the reporting was on the unusual step to not give homework in her class, but there were at least two forms of "concrete" practices and policies that were at the heart of her letter—homework and teacher-family communication.

Dear Parents,

After much research this summer, I am trying something new. Homework will only consist of work that your student did not finish during the school day. There will be no formally assigned homework this year.

Research has been unable to prove that homework improves student performance. Rather, I ask that you spend your evenings doing things that are proven to correlate with student success. Eat dinner as a family, read together, play outside, and get your child to bed early.

Thanks.

Mrs. Brandy Young

The level of publicity that this letter received raises important questions. There is a strong case in the professional literature that homework in early grades is not essential to learning, and in fact can be detrimental, so why is one teacher's decision to follow the research and not assign homework news? If no homework in 2nd grade is good teaching practice, why is it so rare? The answer lies in the fact that homework is one of those unexamined classroom practices that has risen to "untouchable" status. The view that homework is good, and therefore good teachers must assign homework, trumps logic, common sense, and educational research. The detrimental aspects of homework for young children, including developmental inappropriateness and creating an "uneven playing field" for students with different access to resources at home, are not considered.

A second unique aspect of Young's letter is the supportive message it sends to families. A quick Google search of "teacher letters to parents" reveals an array of problems with many templates. The message to families is often authoritarian (e.g., giving "homework" to parents, requiring weekly formal reporting by parents of homework or other activities assigned by the teacher) and judgmental (e.g., statements about what "good" parents do). Letters with this kind of tone go beyond being disrespectful; they highlight the disconnect between what teachers and families want. Hoffman (2014) and Miretsky (2014) identify areas of disconnect in their research and note that teachers are more likely to want to focus exclusively on academic classroom performance, while families are interested in a broader range of issues related to their children's education and well-being. Young's letter acknowledges and supports broad views on learning.

Further, typical negative letters often include inconsistent statements such as "We [teachers and families] are a team," when that is clearly not the case. Young's letter provides an example of an authentic team approach. She is treating the parents as adults, and she supports her suggestions (not mandates) with professional information. Student learning and well-being are at the heart of the letter. She is chipping away at the concrete of unchallenged teaching practices and behaviors toward families. I would trust her to teach my roses.

## How Are Students Who "Love School" Also Educationally Disadvantaged by Policies and Practices That Adversely Impact Those Who "Hate School"?

*Gaining a new lens. We do not even feel the weight of which we own, for someone else is carrying it behind us—out of sight, out of mind.*

—student Rachel Sutphin

There are some students who leave K–12 education relatively unscathed by the deep, long-term impact of bias, marginalization, deficit thinking, and policies and practices of school culture. For these students, there are still many costs, both academic and emotional. The above quote by Sutphin (used with permission) is about examining her privilege—the difficulty in seeing privilege, how others carry the impact, how there are often invisible costs for all. Her quote speaks to ways that students who love school (like her) are also educationally disadvantaged by policies and practices that adversely impact others.

## The Cost of Compliance

Much student success in schools is based on compliance. In compliance-based school cultures, successful students are those who learn to be obedient and submissive, often to the detriment of authentic and meaningful learning. Along the path of education, successful students learn to figure out what the teacher wants to hear and how to "say the right thing."

Examples of compliance can be found throughout the curriculum. For example, I see the cost of compliance for students played out every semester in a writing course that I teach. While some students had enriching writing experiences in their K–12 education, most did not. Students report that they loved writing until "school writing" intervened, squelching creativity, curiosity, self-reflection, and enjoyment. Five-paragraph formulaic essays forbidding the personal voice, driven by simplistic "check-list" prompts, and characterized by a lack of meaningful thinking extinguished the voice and value of authentic writing. Undoing what K–12 education does in writing in college classes is challenging and requires careful community building and pedagogical strategies (Rose, Junk, & Sutphin, 2016).

## The Cost of Bearing Witness to Inequity

Sometimes students witness and are impacted by how others are treated. I hear many stories from students about what they saw in their own educational experiences and in their observations in schools as college students. The following example (shared with permission by student Charisse Junk) describes the memory and impact of such an event.

> I hesitantly giggled, then I glanced down at the wooden classroom desk ashamed of myself. Mrs. Vincent, my first-grade teacher, bellowed in laughter. "Did you hear Todd?" she exclaimed, "He said free instead of three." As the class burst into chuckles, I slightly glanced at the straggly haired boy three rows to my left. My unbecoming behavior made my stomach gurgle like a clogged toilet. Deep in my heart, I knew I had been taught by my parents not to laugh at others, but my teacher encouraged the opposite action

from me and my peers. I sat at my desk confused over the situation.

When students witness unfairness directed toward others, it is difficult to process. Students who are privileged in school "get a pass," and often know it. Their stories go like this: "I realized in high school that I could get by with things. If I was late for class, I wouldn't get into trouble with the teacher. I didn't need a hall pass if I was in the halls when I wasn't supposed to be. There were only a few Black kids in my school. This one kid in my class, he was always getting into trouble. But it was for those same things that I didn't get into trouble for. It wasn't fair."

**The Cost of Dissonance**

It is difficult for preservice teachers and educators (who are products of their own schooling) to question school critically, but the often painful dissonance created by observing inequity provides an opportunity for learning. Charisse Junk was deeply affected as a child by the treatment of her classmate. She felt helpless and guilty for not doing anything to intervene. There was dissonance in both her feelings about her teacher and about herself. As a preservice educator, she was able to process the experience from her perspective as an adult. She could begin to see the event in her 1st-grade classroom in the full context of how inequities impact students: their having a permanent record of being "problem students"; the constant spotlight that shines on the minor infractions of being a kid; the shaming, and the crushing assault on the spirit of the day-to-day exposure to undue scrutiny. She realized the lack of accountability for such actions. Dissonance generated from her experience as a child became the catalyst for meaningful analysis as a preservice teacher of structural inequities in school cultures that create environments for bias.

Another type of dissonance in observing inequity is conflating perceptions of self-success in school with success of schools for all. The logic of assumptions that school "got it right for me; therefore, it gets it right for everyone," or "I am good because school said so; therefore, school is good" is human. Beliefs are shaped by experiences, and if our experiences with school were good, we are less likely to be aware of the limiting aspects of school for others. There is a psychological disincentive to see school as "getting it wrong," because "if I critically question school, then maybe school was wrong about me."

### The Cost of Loss of Autonomy for Teachers

As noted elsewhere, school policies about discipline, attendance, and tardiness, among others, have gotten more punitive and rigid. Teachers have lost autonomy in curricular and human matters in their relationships with students. The impact on teachers is loss of morale, and teacher attrition is consequently high.

An example that illustrates the impact of loss of teacher autonomy on students is the contrast in experiences of two of my current teacher education students. Each planned to visit their former schools during spring break. One was from a suburban school at which her mother taught. The other was from an urban school. The first student was welcomed into the school, and she assisted her mother for a few days. The students in the classroom were thrilled to meet and talk to a college student. The second student was denied access to her high school, where she hoped to see a teacher she had during a two-year teaching professions curriculum, and where she had planned to talk to current students in the program. Her school had a "no former students allowed" policy that granted the teacher no flexibility in making a case for her visit. He couldn't see her, and his students, many of whom see college as financially out of reach, lost an opportunity to talk to a peer about her college experience.

## Why Do Student Feelings about School Remain Unexamined in Many Schools and Teacher Education Programs?

*It is not systematic education which somehow molds society, but, on the contrary, society which, according to its particular structure, shapes education in relation to the ends and interests of those who control the power in that society.*

—Paulo Freire

Freire's observation that society shapes education (rather than the other way around) captures the essence of why student feelings about school are not considered and why educational inequities remain unexamined. Schools are socially constructed spaces. What schools are and how they operate are the result of complex historical, political, economic, and social factors, but those influences in school cultures are rarely explored within schools. There are many conflicting perspectives regarding what the purpose of school is— to train people for the workforce; to "build" democratic citizens; to provide content for life skills; and to nurture love of learning, creativity, and curiosity, among others. The policies and practices of schools reflect whatever the dominant purposes are. A recent example in my state (Ohio) was a proposal by the governor to require teachers to complete professional development "externships" in local businesses or chambers of commerce as part of relicensing requirements, with the intention of having teachers better understand the needs of the workforce. The proposal was included as a provision in the governor's budget. (See Join the Future, 2017, for the full language of the provision.) An additional proposal was to require the appointment of at least three members from the business community on all of the state's 600 school boards. Clearly, the governor sees the primary purpose of school as training the workforce.

Despite controversy over the purposes of schools, schools are universally viewed as places of learning. But what kind of learning should occur (and why) is controversial, debated, and, as Freire noted, societally driven. At present, standardized tests and the corporatization of education are two interrelated examples of how learning is increasingly defined by external forces. In a recent publication, I described how such forces have contributed to "reductionism" in both what is learned and how learning occurs and is measured (Rose, 2014). It is difficult to tell what the future will hold—the pushback against standardized tests and corporatization as detrimental is widespread, but the opposition is powerful.

How school culture contributes to students loving or hating school is largely unexamined in schools, preservice teacher education, and curricular standards and mandates. A lack of attention to the previous assumption— that schools are socially constructed spaces—is a major factor in the lack of examination of school cultures. The presumption is that if something has been traditionally used (and is therefore right and normative), it does not need to be examined. As noted earlier, whether students thrive in, endure, or leave school is generally regarded as a student choice, rather than a result of systemic factors in the culture of schools. The prevailing belief in many schools—one that is shared by many teachers and administrators—is that students who care and work hard will do well; if students are not doing well, it is because they don't care or are not working hard. This belief, although counter to considerable literature on educational equity, allows those in schools to ignore their role in students loving or hating school.

The absence in teacher education of a critical and in-depth examination of educational policies and practices sends a powerful message of deficit thinking. As noted earlier, even for students who "fit" in their K–12 experiences, there are consequences, such as diminished curricula, that lead to a reduction in critical thinking, understanding contexts, and creativity. Curricular standards and mandates generally focus on content and skills rather than systemic factors and educational equity in schools, which is another contributor to lack of attention to the latter. Assessments such as Common Core standards in K–12 education and program accreditation in teacher education, most notably the Council for the Accreditation of Educator Preparation (CAEP), do not adequately focus on issues of educational equity. As schools become more standards-driven and corporatized in the current political climate, the reductive nature of standards will further distance the human dimensions of schooling.

## What Are Strategies to Dismantle Barriers to "Loving School"?

*We can't solve problems by using the same kind of thinking we used when we created them.*

—Albert Einstein

As Einstein's quote suggests, the problem of children and youth "hating school," and the long-lasting consequences and impact on young lives, requires a fresh look. This chapter has highlighted several kinds of thinking that contribute to disregarding how and why students love or hate school. These include the kind of deficit thinking that blames educational outcomes on children, families, or communities, and limits responsibilities of schools; not considering the impact of political, economic, and social factors on what happens in school; a lack of emphasis on the impact of unconscious bias, marginalization, and cultural responsiveness in teaching; and a lack of salience of the issue for many educators and teacher education students whose experiences in schools were positive.

I believe that teacher education is the key to authentic and sustainable change, so I will focus on broad strategies that can empower preservice teachers and assist them in critical thinking and seeing themselves as intellectuals. These strategies can also be adapted for use in professional development or self-learning in schools by teachers and administrators.

**Use the personal stories from preservice teachers' experiences in education.** Know that most students come out of many years of education "liking" or "disliking" schools, but with little examination of why. Assist students in using their own experiences to "dig deeper" in connections to educational equity and to explore the impact of their own identities on their students.

**Empower preservice teachers with knowledge and strategies to build authentic relationships with students and families.** Include concepts such as unconscious bias and deficit thinking in the curriculum (as they have deep impact), and infuse those concepts in class content and field observations throughout the curriculum.

**Examine school practices and policies critically and deeply.** Consider these questions: Who benefits and who does not benefit? What is the purpose? What are unintended consequences? What is the scholarship around a particular issue? Is it connected to or disconnected from traditional practice?

**Give students practice in articulating the pedagogy behind practice.** The era of mandated standards discourages teacher thinking and planning. Teacher education students get little practice in creating standards or evaluating the rationale for existing standards. This limits skill-building in evaluating options and makes them susceptible to accepting poorly developed curricula. Teacher education students need to articulate their own pedagogy so they can develop skills in questioning practices and identifying those that are problematic.

**Incorporate relevant professional reading and current events.** Students need experience in seeing important connections between theory and practice if they are to make those connections as teachers. Readings provide depth in content and an awareness of the range of ways that issues are addressed by authors. Current events show the ways that political, economic, and social factors intersect with education.

**Use writing to enhance depth of learning.** When students write, there is an opportunity for them to expand their thinking, incorporate multiple perspectives, and grapple with complex issues. Learning through writing (when the writing incorporates and values personal voice and analysis of ideas) is different from learning for tests; it is interactive and personal.

## A Final Thought

A small plaque on President Barack Obama's desk in the Oval Office read, "Hard things are hard." There is little doubt that education is hard. It is complex and messy, fraught with challenges, and deeply impactful for individuals, families, communities, and societies. There is much work to do, and the responsibility for doing it falls on educators and allies. We are the sentries who must bear witness and remain vigilant in our challenging and questioning what is not in the best interests of our children—that is, dismantling the concrete surrounding our roses.

As I write these last words, I stop and take a moment, closing my eyes. I imagine a future where someone, maybe my baby granddaughter, holds a newborn of her own and says, "I am so happy for what school is going to do to you."

## References

Boutte, G. (2016). *Educating African-American students: And how are the children?* New York: Routledge.

Delpit, L. (2006). *Other people's children: Cultural conflict in the classroom.* New York: New Press.

Dignity in Schools. *What is school pushout?* Retrieved from http://www.dignityinschools.org/files/Pushout_Fact_Sheet.pdf

Duncan-Andrade, J. (2009). Note to educators: Hope required when growing roses in concrete. *Harvard Educational Review, 79*(2), 181–194.

Duncan-Andrade, J. (2011). *Growing roses in concrete.* TEDxGoldenGate ED. Retrieved from https://www.youtube.com/watch?v=2CwS60ykM8s

Earl, J. (2016). *Second-grade teacher's unique homework policy goes viral.* CBS News. Retrieved from http://www.cbsnews.com/news/second-grade-teachers-unique-homework-policy-goes-viral/

Freire, P. (1970). *Pedagogy of the oppressed.* New York: Herder and Herder.

Gorski, P.C. (2011). Unlearning deficit ideology and the scornful gaze: Thoughts on authenticating the class discourse in education. In P. Gorski & T. Montaño (Eds.), *Assault on kids: How hyper-accountability, corpora-*

*tization, deficit ideology, and Ruby Payne are destroying our schools* (pp. 152–176). New York: Peter Lang.

Heitzeg, N.A. (2016). *The school-to-prison pipeline: Education, discipline, and racialized double standards*. Santa Barbara, CA: Praeger.

Hoffman, L. (2014). Challenging class-based assumptions: Low-income families' perceptions of family involvement. In P.C. Gorski & J. Landsman (Eds.), *The poverty and education reader* (pp. 207–220). Sterling, VA: Stylus Publishing.

Join the Future. (2017). *Kasich budget calls for teachers to intern with local business as license renewal criteria*. Retrieved from http://www.jointhe future.org/join-the-future/kasich-budget-calls-for-teachers-to-intern-with-local-businesses-as-license-renewal-criteria

Kirkland, D.E. (2008). The rose that grew from concrete: Postmodern Blackness and new English education. *The English Journal, 97*(5), 69–75.

Ladson-Billings, G. (2009). *The dreamkeepers: Successful teachers of African-American children*. San Francisco, CA: Jossey-Bass.

Laura, C.T. (2014). *Being bad: My baby brother and the school-to-prison pipeline*. New York: Teachers College Press.

League of Education Voters Foundation. (2011). *School pushout: Dropout and discipline*. Retrieved from http://educationvoters.org/wp-content/uploads/2012/11/White-paper-discipline-010612.pdf

Miretsky, D. (2014). The communication requirements of democratic schools: Parent-teacher perspectives on their relationships. *Teachers College Record, 106*(4), 814–851.

National Association for the Advancement of Colored People (NAACP), Legal Defense Fund. (2017). *School to prison pipeline*. Retrieved from http://www.naacpldf.org/case/school-prison-pipeline

Rose, B. (2014). The big "O": Occupying against reductionism in education using small and sustained actions. In J.A. Gorlewski, D.A. Gorlewski, J. Hopkins, & B.J. Porfilio (Eds.), *Effective or wise? Teaching and the meaning of professional dispositions in education* (pp. 135–154). New York: Peter Lang.

Rose, B., Junk, C., & Sutphin, R. (2016, November). *Do no (more) harm: Undoing the impact of K–12 writing in a university advanced writing class.* Presentation at the 2016 Lilly Conference on College Teaching, Oxford, OH.

Scruggs, A.-O. (2009). Colorblindness: The new racism? *Teaching Tolerance, 36.* Retrieved from http://www.tolerance.org/magazine/number-36-fall-2009/feature/colorblindness-new-racism

Shakur, T. (2000). The rose that grew from concrete. On *The Rose That Grew from Concrete Vol. 1* [CD]. USA: Interscope.

# CHAPTER FOUR

# "WHAT DO YOU THINK WE COULD CHANGE TO MAKE THIS LESSON BETTER?"

## Using Feedback Surveys to Engage Students and Improve Instruction

IRENE S. LaROCHE AND ROBERT W. MALOY

> *When I give surveys to students, I tell them that I rely on them every semester, every year, to give me feedback in order to grow as a teacher. There are some things that I can't do better if they don't tell me.*
> —Sarah Brown Wessling, National Teacher of the Year, 2010

### Introduction

*H*OW TO TALK *So Teens Will Listen & Listen So Teens Will Talk* was the first in a series of books by Adele Faber and Elaine Mazlish (2006) focusing on ways for adults to build more positive communications with children and adolescents. Using self-help exercises and strategies, the authors seek to help adults understand what younger individuals are feeling and saying through their words and actions. Teenagers, but really all young people, "need to be able to express their doubts, confide their fears, and explore options with a grown-up who will listen to them nonjudgmentally and help them make responsible decisions" (Faber & Mazlish, 2006, p. xvii).

Written for parents, the "Talk to Kids" books identify important communication and engagement challenges facing classroom teachers, particularly middle and high school educators, many of whom teach 100 or more students every week. The authors urge parents to "tune in to" what children are experiencing; to put themselves in "children's shoes"; to "accept, rather than deny what children are saying or feeling" (Faber & Mazlish, 2012, p. 3).

But how can classroom teachers connect so directly with classes of 20 to 30 young learners? One-to-one conversations and interactions are not possible with every individual student; teachers need other mechanisms to communicate with students and for students to communicate with them.

In this chapter we discuss the results of a six-year project underway in the College of Education at the University of Massachusetts Amherst, where new history teacher candidates are using feedback surveys to learn how middle and high school students are responding to their instructional methods in the classroom. In this initiative, called the "Conferring with Students" project, teacher candidates design their own survey questionnaires, often with input from students, and they administer them at least four times during the school year. After the surveys have been completed by the students, candidates analyze the data and then discuss the results with students in class. Survey results and teacher/student conversations regularly lead to candidates making student-inspired changes in teaching methods and classroom routines.

The Conferring with Students approach has had a significant impact for both teachers and students. For the teacher candidates, the process of gathering and responding to feedback has provided a unique view of what their classes look like from the other side of the desk, through students' eyes, often revealing previously unknown perspectives and reactions. For most students, the feedback surveys represent the first time they have been asked which teaching methods work well for them as learners—and why. Adults and adolescents alike find that conferring together affords opportunities to talk, listen, and create more positive classroom cultures and learning experiences.

## Student Feedback Surveys: An Emerging Trend

Student feedback surveys are an emerging trend in K–12 education, connected in many districts to efforts to measure and improve teacher effectiveness. In 2014, more than one million 3rd- to 12th-graders completed feedback surveys developed by educational testing companies, and many more youngsters answered state and locally written questionnaires (Bouffard, 2015). Thirty-three states permit using student survey data as part of annual evaluations of K–12 teachers, and seven others—Connecticut, Georgia, Hawaii, Iowa, Kentucky, Massachusetts, and Utah—require that student feedback surveys be collected yearly for teacher evaluation purposes (National Council on Teacher Quality, 2016; Doherty & Jacobs, 2015).

College and university educators are also integrating student feedback surveys into the preparation of new teachers. In Massachusetts, beginning with the 2016–2017 school year, all teacher license candidates are required to gather feedback from students using a model survey instrument provided by the state's Department of Elementary and Secondary Education. Candidates can also receive comments from students in the open response section of the feedback survey. Student survey responses are one of the required categories of evidence (along with student learning growth, classroom observations, artifacts of practice, and progress toward a professional learning goal) that public school mentor teachers and college teacher license program supervisors use to determine a candidate's readiness to receive a license to teach (Massachusetts Department of Elementary and Secondary Education, 2016).

The use of student feedback surveys at the national level was launched in 2009 as part of the Bill & Melinda Gates Foundation–funded Measures of Effective Teaching (MET) Project (2010, 2012, 2013). Begun as an effort to identify what constitutes effective teaching in K–12 schools, the MET project asked more than 100,000 students in six large school systems—Charlotte-Mecklenburg, Dallas, Denver, Hillsborough County, Memphis, and New York City—about their experiences with teachers and schools. By the end of its three-year study, MET researchers concluded that it is possible to identify effective teachers using a combination of student feedback surveys, classroom observations, and student achievement test score gains.

Since 2013, states and school districts have moved aggressively to implement the Measures of Teaching project model, including student feedback surveys. Advocates believe that student survey results correlate with student achievement gains and thus are a method for distinguishing more effective teachers from less effective teachers (LaFee, 2014; Phillips, 2013). Critics counter that students lack full knowledge of curriculum requirements, classroom management expectations, and educational policy decisions that impact the work of teachers. Accordingly, student feedback should not be used as part of teacher evaluation procedures (Dretzke, Sheldon, & Lim, 2014; Hanover Education, 2013, p. 12).

## Feedback Surveys in the Conferring with Students Project

The Conferring with Students project began in 2011 as part of coursework in the History Teacher License program at our university. The goal was to encourage new history teacher candidates to use more student-centered, inquiry-based teaching methods with students. History teaching in K–12 schools is dominated by teacher-centered instructional practices that emphasize students listening to lectures, taking notes on PowerPoint presentations, reading text-based primary sources, and taking tests designed to assess information recall (Cuban, 1993, 2009, 2016).

To challenge this predominant pedagogy, we asked candidates to use best practice instructional methods during the teaching internship (also called student teaching) portion of their license program. "Best practice" means instructional approaches that are "student-centered, active, experiential, authentic, democratic, collaborative, rigorous, and challenging" (Zemelman, Daniels, & Hyde, 2012, p. 2). It can include interactive discussions, groupwork, cooperative learning, primary source analysis, writing, literature, dialog/debate about controversial issues, service learning, role-plays, simulations, research, and technology—in effect, "anything course-related that all students in a class session are called upon to do other than simply watching, listening and taking notes" (Felder & Brent, 2009, p. 2).

As an assignment in one of their master's degree/teacher license courses, candidates initially identified two different best practice, student-centered teaching methods: a "comfort" method (an instructional approach the candidate was confident using with students) and a "reach method" (an instructional approach the candidate was not confident using with students). They then designed lessons featuring each method. Once the lesson had been taught, candidates gave feedback surveys about each method to students in at least one of the history/social studies classes they taught (Maloy & LaRoche, 2015).

In asking candidates to conduct surveys, we imagined that by gaining feedback from students, candidates might be more willing to implement interactive, student-centered instructional approaches in daily lessons. We assumed that student feedback in survey form would intensely interest the teacher candidates who would want to know what middle and high school students thought about them as teachers. And even though most candidates told us they regularly received feedback from students through in-class discussions, end-of-class exit tickets, observations of individual and group learning behaviors, and one-on-one conversations, none of those forms of feedback focus specifically on how students are responding to a teacher's use of different types of instructional practices.

The use of feedback surveys in the Conferring with Students project was very different from the ways in which student questionnaires are being implemented nationally in state- and school district–mandated school reform initiatives (see Table 1).

TABLE 1. Differences in Student Feedback Surveys

| National Student Perception Surveys | Conferring with Students Project Surveys |
| --- | --- |
| Mandated | Voluntary |
| Once a Year at the End of the School Year | Ongoing Throughout the School Year |
| Results May Not Be Discussed with Students | Results Always Discussed with Students |
| Used for Teacher Evaluation | Used for Teacher Professional Development |
| Predesigned Questions from State or District | Teacher-Written Questions |
| Focus on General Student Attitudes | Focus on Specific Teaching Methods |
| Changes Impact Future Students | Changes Impact Current Students |
| Purchased by Schools | Free |

In the Conferring with Students project, candidates designed their own surveys rather than using predeveloped instruments available from testing companies or state education agencies. Candidates surveyed classes while they were teaching them rather than waiting until the end of the school year. Changes to instructional practices could then impact the students currently being taught by the candidates. Candidates solicited feedback about "comfort" and "reach" teaching methods. Candidates discussed with the students both survey results and changes they intended to make because of what students said in the surveys. Candidates gathered student input and made changes in instructional practices in real time, within a framework that emphasized their personal professional development rather than high-stakes results of success or failure. Finally, no candidate's course grade or teacher license evaluation was higher or lower because of how students commented on their teaching practices.

### What the Students Tell the Teachers

Over a period of six years, 142 history teacher candidates collected survey information about classroom instructional methods from more than 4,000 middle and high school students. They surveyed students in at least one of their classes on four occasions—twice when they used a comfort method and twice when they used a reach method. Many candidates conducted surveys multiple times in multiple classes throughout the second half of the school year.

How did students respond to invitations to give survey feedback to their teachers about instructional practices and classroom routines? When the Conferring with Students project first began, some veteran teachers suggested that students would not take the idea seriously by writing sarcastic, mean-spirited, or silly responses to the questions. In fact, the opposite happened. Over the six years of the project, there have been very few instances (fewer than 10 out of more than 4,000 surveys collected) where students dismissed the surveys. Instead, in every class at every grade level from grades 5 to 12, and for every teacher candidate, students responded to the surveys in a serious manner.

Many students gave brief answers to teacher candidates' questions, focusing on what they liked about the class or the teacher as a person. Such comments were expressed in short sentences or phrases. However, between one-quarter and one-third of the surveys received longer comments (two or more sentences) in response to teacher questions. These more in-depth comments usually focused on what the teacher was doing well instructionally, along with suggestions for what the teacher might do to improve the classroom experience for students. Table 2 shows examples of this pattern with a set of responses from students to candidates.

TABLE 2. High School Student Comments on a Teacher
Candidate Written Feedback Survey

Comment 1: "R is a good teacher who makes sure everyone is involved in the lesson. The lessons are fun and interesting. Could do a little better with managing time with the lessons. I learn a lot."

Comment 2: "Your teaching makes class fun and interactive. It's really fun. Something to change is not to go so fast after explaining the material. Give an extra minute to finish writing notes."

Comment 3: "Class is very interesting and informative. Give some more time for notes and allow us some conversation. Allow 30-second break after taking down all the notes. Good notes, maybe less if you can."

Comment 4: "It would be more beneficial if we did other activities like worksheets or packets, rather than always paying attention and taking notes. I also believe R should relax a bit more because we want to pay attention more when R relaxes rather than being uptight all the time."

The length and depth of responses by students varied depending on how candidates chose to ask feedback questions. When questions were phrased in general terms, students gave general answers. For example, the question "What do you like about working in groups while doing class work?" generated mostly short, non-specific responses such as "I like groups" or "I don't like groups." By contrast, the question "How did groupwork and an in-class simulation help you understand the Electoral College?" received more specific responses that included insights from students about the role of the states in elections or how a candidate does not have to win the popular vote to be elected president.

To support students in giving more specific feedback, we suggested that candidates organize surveys using an ideas/issues/insights format. In this approach, candidates would ask students for their *ideas* (in what other ways would you like to see this method used?), *issues* (what difficulties did you have with this method?), and *insights* (how did this method help you learn?). An ideas/issues/insights approach moved the focus away from asking whether students "liked" or "enjoyed" a teaching method and toward emphasizing what students learned or remembered from the instructional experience.

### How the Teachers Respond to Feedback

At the outset, most teacher candidates expressed reluctance about soliciting survey feedback from an entire class of students. One candidate spoke for many of his peers when he said that asking students for feedback was at first "nerve-wracking." Candidates worried that students would not take the survey questions seriously or that they would offer uninformative feedback. Some candidates worried that asking students for feedback would undermine their perceived position of authority in the classroom. Still others expressed concern that students would be disappointed if teaching approaches or classroom routines did not "change exactly as they had hoped."

Initial reluctance aside, candidates began reconsidering instructional practices based on student feedback. After reading responses about a jigsaw activity where students were asked to read pro- and anti-imperialism articles in a U.S. history class and then share what they learned in small groups, a high school candidate learned that students almost unanimously found the primary sources difficult to understand. The teacher concluded that she had to change her approach, stating: "In the future, I will make sure that I give my students more background knowledge…. I will choose the articles more carefully and either pick easier articles or cut them down more."

During a lesson on women activists of the 1920s, students at another high school also found primary sources "confusing," "hard to understand," and "worded weirdly." The students offered numerous suggestions for improvement, including "read all the documents together," "do more visual things," and "make it [primary source materials] more interactive." The teacher agreed, saying that "the feedback has encouraged me and pushed me to use students' ideas in the classroom. This way, classroom activities are created by both the students and the teachers."

Feedback from students sometimes served to confirm for candidates the value of a teaching method. A high school candidate had students use art to construct a visual timeline depicting specific events in the history of American westward expansion. The timelines had to be completed in a rushed manner due to another activity running long, and the candidate was worried that students would disparage the activity. Although many students commented that they did not have enough time to finish their timelines, there were many positive responses to the approach. Students said that drawing helped them visualize the events and remember the historical information. The teacher noted: "I appreciate how valuable the method of art truly is.... [I]t gives students space to do some higher order thinking by engaging their creative sides."

Each year, candidates made immediate changes to instructional practices and classroom routines based on what the students said in their feedback surveys. After completing a research paper in which students had to offer evidence in support of their assessment of the most important accomplishment of George Washington's presidency, they wanted more ways to present their findings. One student suggested "mak[ing] pictures obligatory to illustrate events." Another asked for "more choices on how to do the project." The teacher agreed and incorporated those ideas into the next research paper assignment.

A middle school candidate did a writer's workshop activity in which students in groups of three gave peer feedback to each other's drafts on an essay topic, "How can someone justify war?" In their feedback surveys, students said they enjoyed the workshop format, liked seeing different writing styles, and appreciated hearing comments from classmates, but they wanted more time to discuss and provide feedback. The students also suggested that peer feedback would be a good way to examine DBQs (document-based questions). The teacher agreed and resolved to integrate both ideas into future lessons.

In some cases, candidates incorporated suggestions from individual students into the larger class format. One student wrote that she wanted more about Black history and slavery; the candidate subsequently noted, "I have been including more African American history." Another student in that same class wanted to see more role plays; the candidate decided to use a "reader's theatre for the visual and audio learners in the classroom." When a third student wrote that she did not like a groupwork project because she and her partner had wasted time in class and then she had to do all the work at the last minute, the candidate had a productive conversation with the girls about using "class time to its fullest and choosing partners wisely."

By the end of the school year, nearly all the candidates endorsed using feedback surveys as a feature of their teaching practice. A middle school teacher candidate declared, "I think it [a feedback survey] builds a good relationship with students because they feel their opinions are being heard." A high school colleague concurred: "I think that it is important for students to know they have a voice in how they learn, and that their teacher cares about their feedback to help improve their teaching."

Surveys gave candidates unique perspectives on their work in the classroom, for, as a high school teacher noted, "Up until this project, I hadn't had the chance to really look at what teaching methods my students enjoy, and more importantly what they are taking away from my lessons." Another high school candidate said, "I was forced to really evaluate how the lessons went and embrace the negatives as well as the positives." A middle school candidate echoed many of her peers when she declared, "I believe that receiving feedback is a crucial aspect of teaching. Since using the feedback forms, I have encouraged students to provide me with feedback when they feel it is necessary."

## Feedback as an Engagement and Improvement Approach

While, as we noted, the size of the Conferring with Students project is small—some 4,000 middle and high school students in classes taught by 142 new teacher candidates over the past six years—its implications are broad, reaching beyond a single initiative to inform wider discussions about the most effective ways for teachers and students to use feedback surveys to communicate with one another about how teaching and learning are happening in their classrooms.

Based on the project results, we offer the following conclusions about how feedback surveys can impact student engagement and teaching practices.

### 1. Engaging Students with School

Lack of student engagement is a crisis in schools today, with many youngsters feeling disconnected and discouraged by teacher-directed classroom learning. When asked as part of the 2013/2014 High School Surveys of Student Engagement, 56% of the students disagreed or strongly disagreed with the statement "I go school because I enjoy being in school." Only half of public school students agreed or strongly agreed with the statement "In general, I am excited about my classes." When comparing students from different types of schools, 86% of public school students and 82%

of independent school students said they were sometimes or often bored in class (National Association of Independent Schools, 2015).

Student engagement "refers to the degree of attention, curiosity, interest, optimism, and passion that students show when they are learning or being taught, which extends to the level of motivation they have to learn and progress in their education" (The Glossary of Education Reform, 2016). To create greater engagement, researchers urge active teaching and learning featuring group work and projects, high expectations for everyone to work hard and learn, and activities designed by instructors to help students build connections between the curriculum and their personal lives and interests (Finley, 2015; Zemelman et al., 2012).

Regular use of teacher-written student feedback surveys can be added to the list of ways for teachers to more fully engage students with school. Based on reflection papers written by teacher candidates and an analysis of student responses to survey questions, across the six years of the project, students overwhelmingly took the surveys seriously, providing answers (however brief) to every question asked by teachers. In many cases, students offered specific and substantive ideas for improving teaching methods and classroom routines. Repeatedly, candidates told us how students welcomed the opportunity to share their thoughts on the feedback surveys. In classrooms, the process of asking for and collecting feedback, talking with students about what they said, and then making shifts and changes to instructional practices and daily routines impacted the mood and climate of the class in positive ways. Candidates believed that students were more involved with their classes because their ideas and opinions were being solicited and listened to by their teacher.

## 2. Changing Teaching Practices

How teachers teach is a continuing issue in how students think about their school experiences. Historian Larry Cuban (1993, 2016) has documented a longstanding conflict between teacher-centered and student-centered visions of how best to organize classrooms for learning. Cuban suggests that while most teachers express a desire to be more student-centered in their teaching, they also face intense pressure from administrators and parents to raise student test scores using teacher-centered instructional methods. As a result, many teachers are reluctant to try new approaches to instruction and instead are left "hugging the middle" between teacher-centered and student-centered methods (Cuban, 2009).

Feedback from students gave the teacher candidates in the Conferring with Students project valuable ideas and insights about how to use more interactive, best practice, student-centered teaching methods. For many candidates, feedback provided the confidence they needed to push themselves beyond predominantly teacher-centered instructional practices. Candidates found themselves agreeing with what students had to say about methods and routines, realizing that they needed to slow down their presentations, use more visuals, allow for more individual and small group projects, and vary the types of activities during class time—so they told students that they would make those changes, and they did. They discovered that "reach" teaching methods they had been reluctant to use were often well received by students. That feedback renewed their readiness to continue using those approaches in the future while students saw firsthand that their opinions had been heard and acted upon.

### 3. Democratic Patterns of Communication

Feedback surveys generated communication patterns that did not occur as substantively or as often when teacher candidates used more common types of feedback, such as end-of-class exit tickets or in-class group discussions. In the Conferring with Students project, teacher candidates read the written survey comments, acknowledging what students saw as strengths or said needed to be improved in their teaching practice. Candidates used those surveys as opportunities to stand back from the pressures of planning and teaching daily lessons to think about what was working and what they might do differently in the classroom. Then, based on those reflections and reconsiderations, candidates made changes to instructional practices and classroom routines.

But the surveys alone were not the full basis for new patterns of classroom communications in the Conferring with Students project. Candidates also talked with students about what was said on the surveys—that is, teacher and students had to confer together as a class. Conferring rests on the democratically inspired idea that for feedback surveys to realize their full potential to engage learners, teachers need to talk with students (and students have to talk with teachers) about survey results and discuss the changes they plan to make—or not make—in response to ideas and suggestions from classes.

It is in the ways that teachers respond to feedback that students realize that their voices are heard, their opinions are respected, and their ideas are part of the classroom community. As one candidate wrote after holding his initial post-survey conversation with his middle school class: "A wall had been broken down between us. No longer was I the distant instructor teaching from way up on high, but instead someone who was just trying to learn and get better, like the students." For the rest of the school year, that candidate shared each set of survey results with the students, and together they discussed the results and changes that could be made to instructional practices and classroom routines. Conferring became a regular part of the classroom; the students even cheered when told they had another survey to complete. Providing feedback, the candidate concluded, "is one of the only times that they [students] have a say in the ways that their class and therefore their day is constructed."

Through the Conferring with Students project, written feedback surveys designed by teachers and shared with students served as a tool for making substantive communication take place between adults and young learners in school classrooms. For teachers, surveys are a form of talk, a means of shared communication, a window onto the ideas and reactions of students to their daily school experiences. For students, surveys offer opportunities to share what they are thinking and to feel listened to by their teachers. From this foundation, more engaged and productive learning in more open and inclusive classroom communities can surely follow.

## References

Bouffard, S. (2015, May-June). Learning from our students: Surveys offer performance feedback to teachers. *Harvard Education Letter, 31*(3), 1, 6.

Cuban, L. (1993). *How teachers taught: Constancy and change in American classrooms, 1890–1990.* New York: Teachers College Press.

Cuban, L. (2009). *Hugging the middle: How teachers teach in an era of testing and accountability.* New York: Teachers College Press.

Cuban, L. (2016). *Teaching history then and now: A story of stability and change in schools.* Cambridge, MA: Harvard University Press.

Doherty, K.M., & Jacobs, S. (2015, November). *State of the states: Evaluating teaching, leading and learning.* Washington, DC: National Council on Teacher Quality.

Dretzke, B.J., Sheldon, T.D., & Lim, A. (2014). What do K–12 teachers think about including student surveys in their performance ratings? *Mid-Western Educational Researcher, 27*(3), 185–206.

Faber, A., & Mazlish, E. (2006). *How to talk so teens will listen & listen so teens will talk.* New York: HarperCollins.

Faber, A., & Mazlish, E. (2012). *How to talk so kids will listen & listen so kids will talk.* New York: Scribner.

Felder, R., & Brent, R. (2009). Active learning: An introduction. *ASQ Higher Education Brief, 2*(4). Retrieved from http://www4.ncsu.edu/unity/lockers/users/f/felder/public/Papers/ALpaper(ASQ).pdf

Finley, T. (2015, September 9). New study: Engage kids with 7x the effect. *Edutopia.* Retrieved from https://www.edutopia.org/blog/engage-with-7x-the-effect-todd-finley

Gallup Inc. (2015, Fall). *Gallup student poll: Engaged today—Ready for tomorrow.* Retrieved from http://www.gallupstudentpoll.com/188036/2015-gallup-student-poll-overall-report.aspx

The Glossary of Education Reform. (2016). *Student engagement: The Great Schools Partnership.* Retrieved from http://edglossary.org/student-engagement/

Hanover Education. (2013, February). Student perception surveys and teacher assessments. Retrieved from http://dese.mo.gov/sites/default/files/Hanover-Research-Student-Surveys.pdf

LaFee, S. (2014, March). Student evaluating teachers. *School Administrator, 71*(3), 15–25.

Maloy, R.W., & LaRoche, I.S. (2015). *We, the students and teachers: Teaching democratically in the history and social studies classroom.* Albany: State University of New York Press.

Massachusetts Department of Elementary and Secondary Education. (2016, June). *Guidelines for the candidate assessment of performance: Assessment of teacher candidates.* Malden, MA: Author.

Measures of Effective Teaching Project. (2010, September). *Student perceptions and the MET project.* Seattle, WA: Bill & Melinda Gates Foundation. Retrieved from http://www.metproject.org/downloads/Student_Perceptions_092110.pdf

Measures of Effective Teaching Project. (2012, January). *Gathering feed-*

*back for teaching: Combining high-quality observations with student surveys and achievement gains.* Seattle, WA: Bill & Melinda Gates Foundation. Retrieved from http://www.metproject.org/downloads/MET_Gathering_Feedback_Practioner_Brief.pdf

Measures of Effective Teaching Project. (2012, May). *Learning about teaching: Initial findings from the Measures of Effective Teaching Project.* Seattle, WA: Bill & Melinda Gates Foundation. Retrieved from http://www.gatesfoundation.org/college-ready-education/Documents/preliminary-finding-policy-brief.pdf

Measures of Effective Teaching Project. (2012, September). *Asking students about teaching: Student perception surveys and their implementation.* Seattle, WA: Bill & Melinda Gates Foundation. Retrieved from http://www.metproject.org/downloads/Asking_Students_Practitioner_Brief.pdf

Measures of Effective Teaching Project. (2013, January). *Ensuring fair and reliable measures of effective teaching: Culminating findings from the MET Project's three-year study.* Seattle, WA: Bill & Melinda Gates Foundation. Retrieved from http://metproject.org/downloads/MET_Ensuring_Fair_and_Reliable_Measures_Practitioner_Brief.pdf

National Association of Independent Schools. (2015, March). *2014 NAIS report on the High School Survey of Student Engagement.* Retrieved from http://headsuped.com/wp-content/uploads/2015/05/HSSSE-NAIS-2014-Report-on-Student-Engagement.pdf

National Council on Teacher Quality. (2016). *2015 state teacher quality policy yearbook: National Summary.* Retrieved from http://www.nctq.org/dmsView/2015_State_Teacher_Policy_Yearbook_National_Summary_NCTQ_Report

Phillips, V. (2013, March). Listening to students: Well-designed student surveys help teachers improve their practice. *Principal Leadership, 13*(7), 40–41.

Zemelman, S., Daniels, H., & Hyde, A. (2012). *Best practice: Bringing standards to life in American classrooms* (4th ed.). Portsmouth, NH: Heinemann.

# CHAPTER FIVE

# FROM THE DESK OF YOUR STUDENT

## Ruminations on School

MEGAN J. SULSBERGER

### A Call to Ruminate

THE LAST BELL RINGS. Rushed goodbyes are exchanged in the hallway as teachers close their doors, eager to begin their next class periods. Thirty-one energetic and somewhat awkward 6th-graders take their seats in a bustling classroom space, some more reluctantly than others. The schedule is posted on the board, but today feels a bit different than the rest.

It doesn't take long for someone to notice: the desktops have been cleared, and there is an extra body in the room. Today isn't a typical day in Ms. I's science class. Blank white paper and freshly sharpened pencils are quickly passed around while eager ears listen on.

"If I were to ask you to share your honest feelings about school, what would you say?"

The students, previously chatty and restless, take pause.

"Is that what these blank papers are for? Like, you want us to share our feelings with you?" one student asks.

"What I want to know is, are these pages going down as anonymous?"

chimes in another. "'Cause there are some things I think people in this world just need to know."

"Who is really gonna read this?" asks a third.

Questions are answered, and ideas are encouraged. Approaches are reaffirmed, and fears are calmed.

Then it happens: the pencils of even the most skeptical and typically disengaged students begin to scratch. The teachers and researcher, with eyebrows raised in surprise, smile at each other from across the now-quiet classroom.

Turns out, these 6th-grade students do have some things to tell us about school.

### The Case for Student Perspectives

This qualitative research project stemmed from a belief that research should be done *with* and *for* students and not just *on* them. To state it simply: *When pondering why kids love or hate school, we should just ask them.* From this place of purpose and with an eye toward equity, this research sought to discover what public school students would share about their school experiences when provided an opportunity to express their feelings.

Narrative inquiry methods were utilized to gather written, visual, and/or oral narratives from 6th-grade students as a means of describing and analyzing particular aspects of their school experiences (Bruner, 1991; Clandinin & Connelly, 2000). A population of 6th-graders was purposefully sampled to capture the witty, angsty voices that slice across human existence—no longer a boy/girl, not yet a man/woman. An unfiltered rawness lies in-between. As the students' expressions were coded to examine trends and themes in the data, the diversity of students' experiences and the messages they hoped to communicate became visible in their work.

What follows is a sampling of diverse narratives that provides an intimate glimpse into a group of students' feelings about school and their surprisingly complicated lives.

### Let the Students Speak

The prompt: "If I were to ask you to share your honest feelings about school, what would you say?"

Sometimes, school can be like a Day at the Beach.

FIGURE 1. 6th-grade male

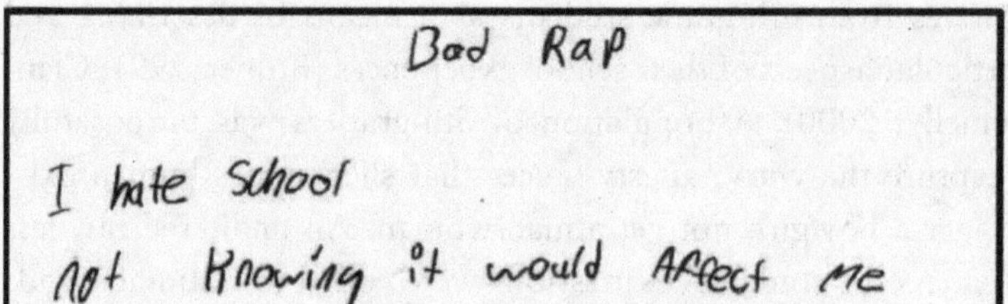

Bad Rap

I hate school
not knowing it would Affect me
ignorance got me blineded
Im hoping the world excepts
me    but I'm nothing Life
the Popular Kids tho.

FIGURE 2. 6th-grade male

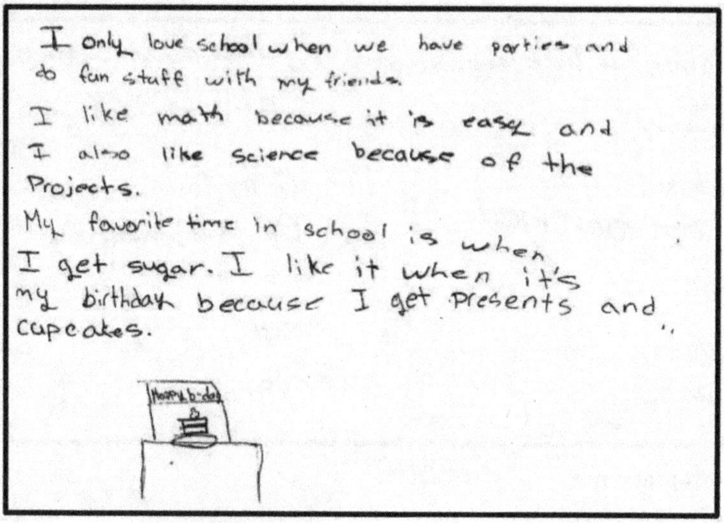

I only love school when we have parties and do fun stuff with my friends.
I like math because it is easy and I also like science because of the Projects.
My favorite time in school is when I get sugar. I like it when it's my birthday because I get presents and cupcakes.

FIGURE 3. 6th-grade male

I Love coming to school because we talk and see our friends. I wish we can do more projects in my other classes because I only do projects in my science class. I also wish we can use the computers more often.

FIGURE 4. 6th-grade female

FIGURE 5. 6th-grade male

FIGURE 6. 6th-grade female

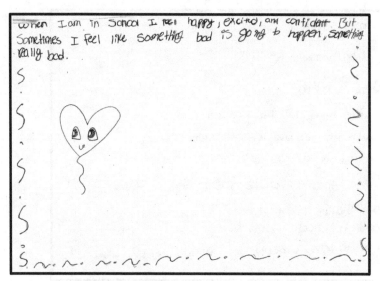

When I am in School I feel happy, excited, and confident. But sometimes I feel like something bad is going to happen, something really bad.

FIGURE 7. 6th-grade female

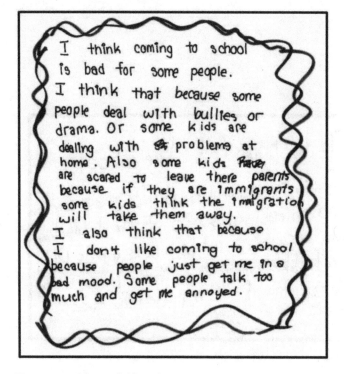

I think coming to school is bad for some people. I think that because some people deal with bullies or drama. Or some kids are dealing with problems at home. Also some kids are scared to leave there parents because if they are immigrants some kids think the immigration will take them away. I also think that because I don't like coming to school because people just get me in a bad mood. Some people talk too much and get me annoyed.

FIGURE 8. 6th-grade female

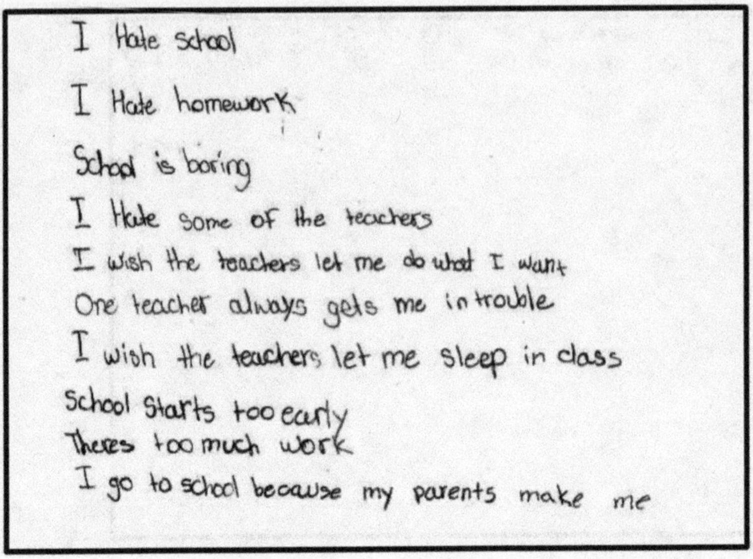

I Hate school

I Hate homework

School is boring

I Hate some of the teachers

I wish the teachers let me do what I want

One teacher always gets me in trouble

I wish the teachers let me sleep in class

School starts too early

Theres too much work

I go to school because my parents make me

FIGURE 9. 6th-grade male

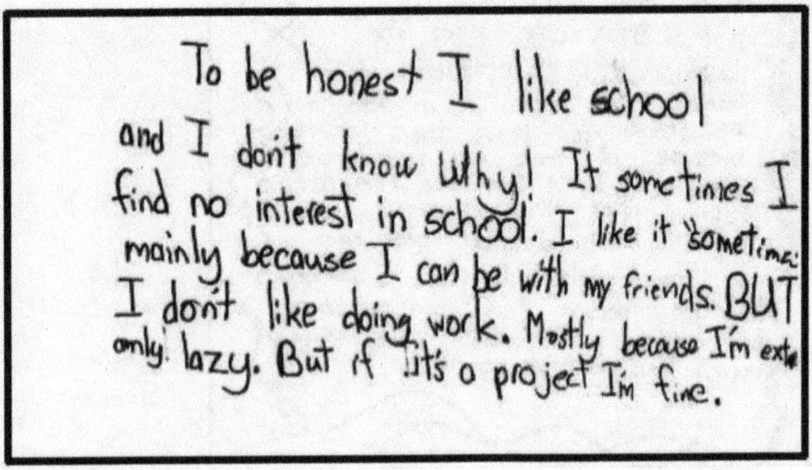

To be honest I like school and I don't know why! It sometimes I find no interest in school. I like it sometime mainly because I can be with my friends. BUT I don't like doing work. Mostly because I'm ext only lazy. But if it's a project I'm fine.

FIGURE 10. 6th-grade male

If you want to experience something cool Jist pack your bags and go to school. If you are feeling sad, Just go to school its not so bad.

FIGURE 11. 6th-grade female

I like my first and second period teach because she explains every thing good but my third and fourth teacher period is so boring it make me yan becau he so boring he is not that good at explain. And my fifth period teacher is Just simple. I would trade for another teacher. But if my third and fourth period teacher is reading I'm sorry but people need to know. And my six period teacher only is calm if she watch baby animals.

FIGURE 12. 6th-grade female

How I feel about school is paper

because everywhere in the school has paper. Like I have to do assignments, homework with paper.

FIGURE 13. 6th-grade male

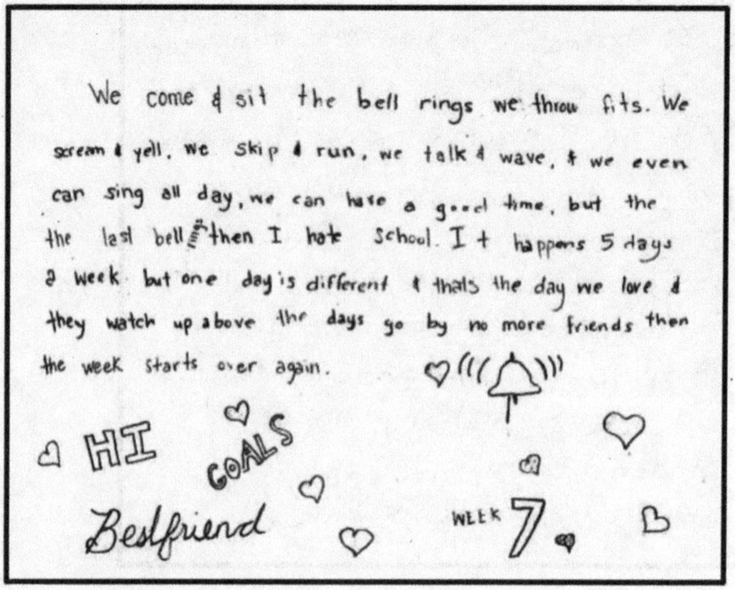

We come & sit the bell rings we throw fits. We scream & yell. we skip & run. we talk & wave, & we even can sing all day, we can have a good time. but the the last bell then I hate school. It happens 5 days a week but one day is different & thats the day we love & they watch up above the days go by no more friends then the week starts over again.

HI GOALS
Bestfriend          WEEK 7

FIGURE 14. 6th-grade female

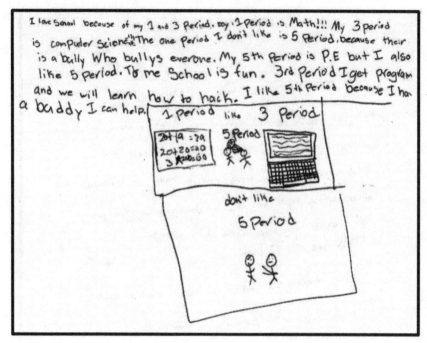

I love school because of my 1 and 3 Period. my 1 period is Math!!! My 3 period is computer Science. The one Period I don't like is 5 Period, because their is a bully who bullys everone. My 5th Period is P.E but I also like 5 period. To me School is fun. 3rd Period I get program and we will learn how to hack. I like 5th Period because I hav a buddy I can help.

1 period       like    3 Period
5 Period

don't like
5 Period

FIGURE 15. 6th-grade male

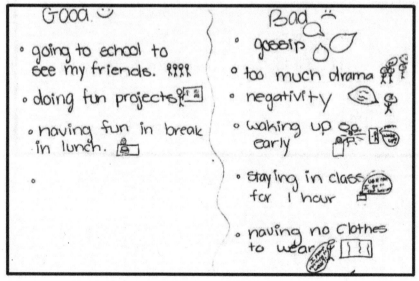

Good.
• going to school to see my friends.
• doing fun projects
• having fun in break in lunch.
•

Bad
• gossip
• too much drama
• negativity
• waking up early
• staying in class for 1 hour
• having no clothes to wear

FIGURE 16. 6th-grade female

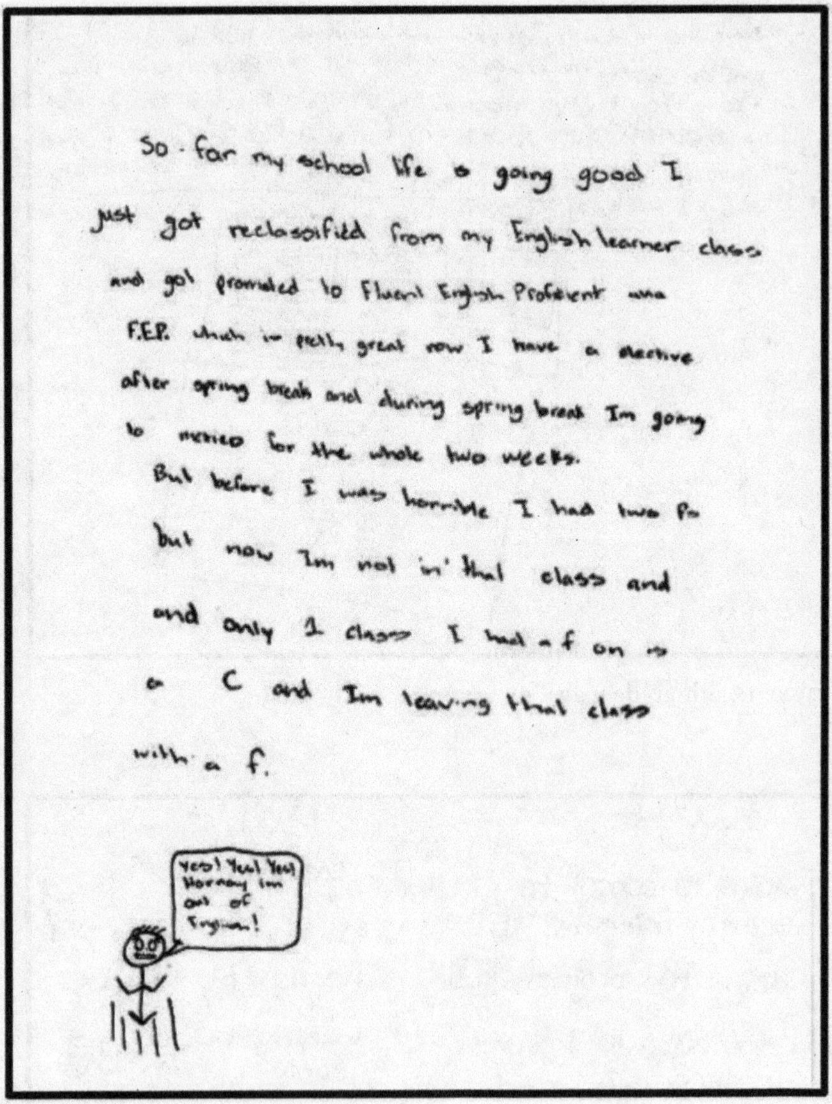

So · far my school life is going good I just got reclassified from my English learner class and got promoted to Fluent English Proficient aka F.E.P. which is really great now I have a elective after spring break and during spring break Im going to mexico for the whole two weeks.
But before I was horrible I had two Fs but now Im not in' that class and and only 1 class I had a f on is a C and Im leaving that class with a f.

FIGURE 17. 6th-grade male

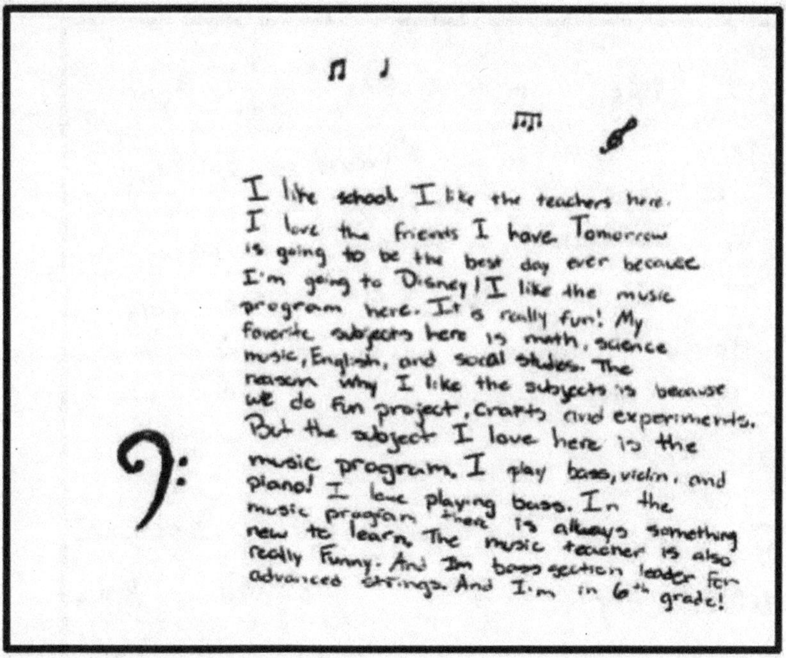

FIGURE 18. 6th-grade female

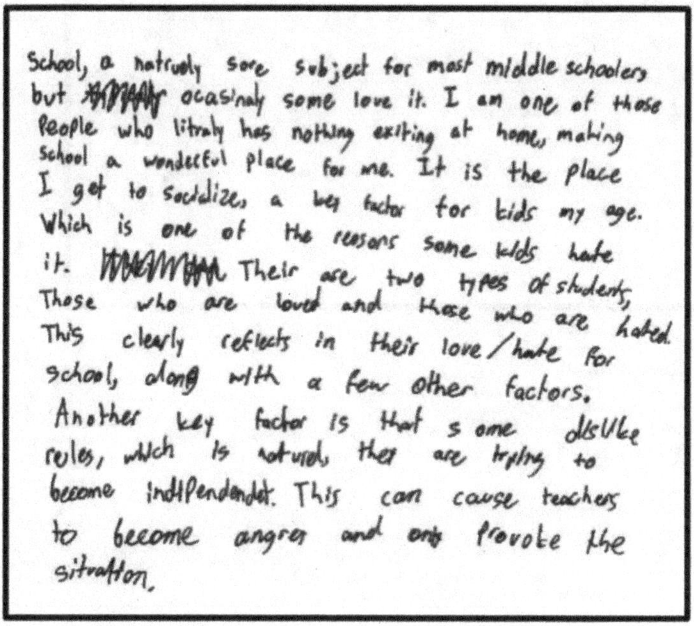

I like school. I like the teachers here. I love the friends I have. Tomorrow is going to be the best day ever because I'm going to Disney! I like the music program here. It's really fun! My favorite subjects here is math, science, music, English, and social studies. The reason why I like the subjects is because we do fun project, crafts and experiments. But the subject I love here is the music program. I play bass, violin, and piano! I love playing bass. In the music program there is always something new to learn. The music teacher is also really funny. And I'm bass section leader for advanced strings. And I'm in 6th grade!

FIGURE 19. 6th-grade male

School, a natruoly sore subject for most middle schoolers but occasinaly some love it. I am one of those people who litroly has nothing exiting at home, making school a wonderful place for me. It is the place I get to socialize, a key factor for kids my age. Which is one of the reasons some kids hate it. Their are two types of students, Those who are loved and those who are hated. This clearly reflects in their love/hate for school, along with a few other factors. Another key factor is that some dislike rules, which is natural, they are trying to become indtpendandt. This can cause teachers to become angrer and only provoke the sitroaton.

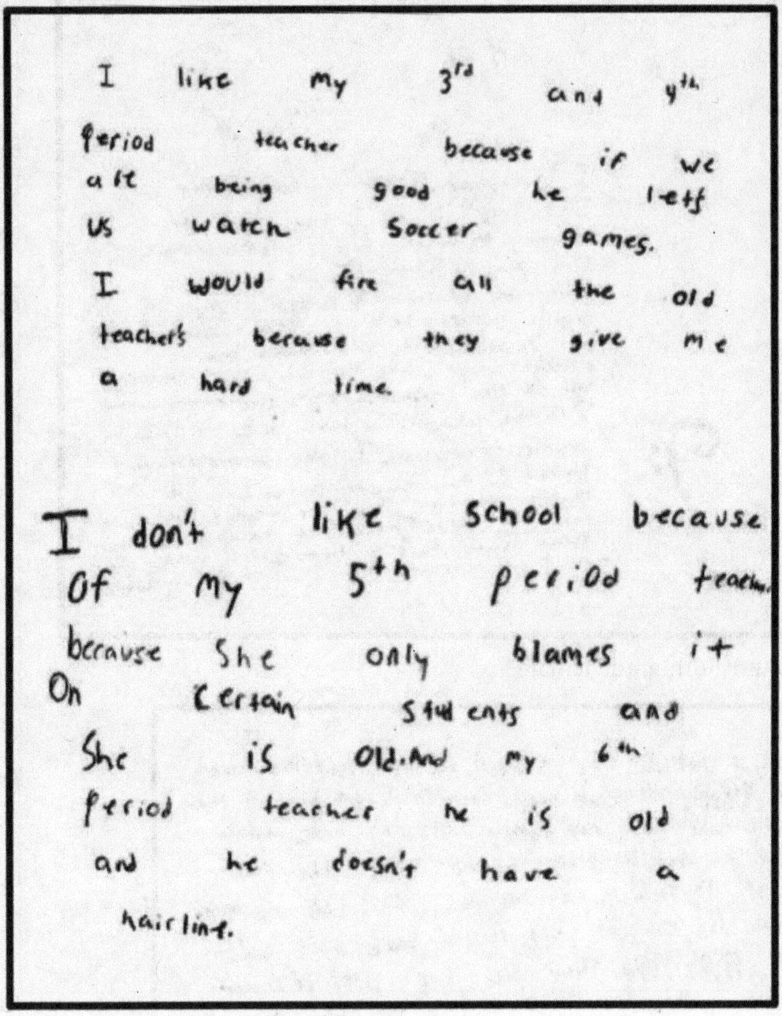

I like my 3rd and 4th
period teacher because if we
are being good he lets
us watch soccer games.
I would fire all the old
teacher's because they give me
a hard time.

I don't like school because
of my 5th period teacher
because she only blames it
on certain students and
she is old. And my 6th
period teacher he is old
and he doesn't have a
hairline.

FIGURE 20. 6th-grade male

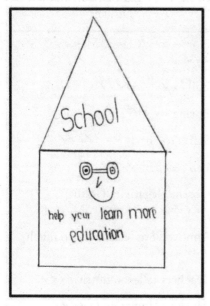

FIGURE 21. 6th-grade male

## So What Exactly Are These Students Trying to Tell Us?

As evidenced in the students' ruminations, these 6th-graders have mixed emotions about their school experiences. While the student in Figure 1 feels that a day at school is like "a day at the beach," others such as the student in Figure 9 "hate" school or find it difficult to be present there for personal reasons. There is much to learn about the lives of students when we take a deeper look at the intended or unintended meanings of their narratives.

Table 1 shows the variety and frequency of factors that students feel contribute to their positive and/or negative school experiences. A response was coded as a "like" if the idea or notion about school expressed by the student was couched in a positive narrative or included an otherwise upbeat message or drawing about school. A response was coded as a "dislike" if the student expressed tones of anger, sadness, or an outward dissatisfaction with a particular aspect of his or her experience. In cases where a drawing or written narrative did not match, or an interpretation was difficult, clarification was sought from the student about the work through an oral narrative. Further, student responses that indicated both positive and negative factors were considered in both categories.

| Likes | Dislikes |
|---|---|
| Friends ✓✓✓✓✓✓✓✓✓✓✓✓✓✓ ✓✓✓✓✓ | Homework/Classwork ✓✓✓✓✓✓ ✓✓✓ |
| Learning ✓✓✓✓✓✓ | Bullies ✓✓✓✓✓✓✓ |
| Good teachers ✓✓✓✓✓✓ | Boring ✓✓✓✓✓✓✓ |
| School subjects | Starts too early ✓✓✓✓✓✓✓ |
| • Math ✓✓✓✓✓ | Bad teachers ✓✓✓✓✓✓ |
| • PE ✓✓✓✓ | Gossip/Negativity/Drama ✓✓✓✓✓✓ |
| • Science ✓✓✓ | |
| • Social Studies ✓✓ | Annoyed/Students talk too much ✓✓✓✓✓✓ |
| • Computers ✓✓ | Teachers talk too much ✓✓✓✓ |
| • English ✓ | Always get in trouble ✓✓✓✓ |
| Projects ✓✓✓ | Lunch food ✓✓✓✓ |
| Break/Lunch break ✓✓✓ | Reading/English ✓✓ |
| Meet new people ✓✓✓ | Home-related issues ✓ |
| Class parties ✓✓ | Teachers don't let me do what I want ✓ |
| Being away from home ✓✓ | |
| Music program ✓ | Not like the popular kids ✓ |
| Moved up from remedial class ✓ | In classes too long ✓ |
| Food ✓ | Not having clothes/knowing what to wear ✓ |
| Staff is nice ✓ | |
| Fun Friday ✓ | It's hard/No help ✓ |
| Like a day at the beach ✓ | Sitting ✓ |
| | Have to bring your own ball ✓ |
| | Uniform ✓ |
| | Too much pressure ✓ |

TABLE 1. Why 6th-Graders Like or Dislike School

As responses were coded, the variety of reasons that students offered for liking or disliking school were then collapsed into three major categories, as shown in Table 2: Academic Reasons, Social Reasons, and Personal Reasons. Academic reasons include all responses specifically pertaining to school itself. Social reasons capture all aspects of the school experience related to students' positive or negative interactions with their peers. Personal reasons encompass all responses that fall outside the other two categories or that are phrased as direct expressions of the self. Responses with a standard "bullet" in front of them fall into the "Likes" category, while responses with the "diamond bullet" fall into the "Dislikes" category.

| Academic Reasons | Social Reasons | Personal Reasons |
|---|---|---|
| • Learning | • Friends | • Being away from home |
| • Good teachers | • Class parties | • Food |
| • Math | • Break/Lunch break | |
| • Science | • Staff is nice | ◊ Annoyed |
| • English | • Fun Friday | ◊ Home-related issues |
| • Social Studies | • Meet new people | ◊ Always getting into trouble |
| • Computers/ Computer Science | ◊ Bullies | ◊ Boring |
| • PE | ◊ Drama | ◊ Don't let me do what I want |
| • Projects | ◊ Others talk too much | |
| • Music program | ◊ Not like the popular kids | ◊ Not having/knowing what to wear |
| • Moved up from remedial class | ◊ Gossip | ◊ Sitting for too long |
| | ◊ Negativity | ◊ Lunch food |
| ◊ Homework/ Classwork | ◊ Other students | ◊ Bring your own ball |
| ◊ Bad teachers | | ◊ Uniform |
| ◊ School starts too early | | |
| ◊ In classes too long | | |
| ◊ It's hard/No help | | |
| ◊ Teachers talk too much | | |
| ◊ Reading/English | | |
| ◊ Too much pressure | | |

TABLE 2. Categories in Student Data: Academic, Social, and Personal Reasons

There were some important themes that emerged throughout the analysis of student data that may enlighten educators during their work with students. These have been termed: Friends Matter Most; Learning Can Be Enjoyable; Bullies Distract and Divide; Fear Prevents Presence; and Teachers Should Care.

## Friends Matter Most

In examining the positive factors from Table 1 more closely, it is no surprise that 6th-graders most frequently reported "friends" as an important reason for loving school. As represented in such Figures as 3–6 and 14, social interactions with peers within the school setting ascribe a certain level of relevance or meaning to these students' school experiences. (Can we not agree that we felt this way once ourselves?) Knowing that we, too, were young and hungry for peer interaction brings a kindred relatability to a teacher's relationship with his or her students—and, I might say, a sense of humor pertaining to these interactions that can yield a certain level of patience necessary to survive a school day. There is an innocence in this response that can soften our interactions. As we come to see a bit of ourselves in our students, they may pick up on this from us and respond differently.

## Learning Can Be Enjoyable

In some students' responses—for example, in Figures 3, 15, 17, 18, and 21—it is refreshing to see a love of learning and subject-specific areas emerging as a top reason students reported enjoying school. Contrary to what we may sometimes feel from our students, they do have an interest in learning and a fascination with particular subject areas. Related to this were specific ways of learning that were valued, such as "projects" or project-based learning experiences (referenced in Figures 4, 10, and 16). Translated into our practice, this calls for more hands-on, real-world learning experiences, as well as more performance-based tasks and assessments. As captured in Figure 13, learning should move beyond the "paper." To quench students' thirst for social experiences inside the classroom, we are reminded again that incorporating group learning experiences into course design or curricula may increase student enjoyment and motivation. In addition, with the knowledge that students have a preference for particular subject areas over others, the integrated nature of learning across subjects and experiences becomes even more important.

## Bullies Distract and Divide

There remains a complicated social structure within schools that lurks behind positive student interactions and beyond the awareness of adults. For the students in this study, negative experiences or instances of bullying during the school day had a startling impact on their feelings about school and their ability to attend to school-related tasks. As mentioned in Figures 6 and 15, experiences with a bully can affect students emotionally or lead them to dislike an entire class period. As teachers, we know what this looks and feels like all too well. Figure 19 bluntly explains that there are two types of students: "Those who are loved and those who are hated." We are called upon to ask and interrogate this notion with our students: Why would anyone be classified as "hated"? While it is complicated to unravel ideas about popularity and acceptance with our students, we must hold firm to the principle that no student should take away from another student's learning or positive experience in our classrooms. It must remain a priority of teachers to disempower bullies and to champion safe spaces for students. As was the case in this project, even discussing the responses wherein instances of bullying were mentioned reminded students of the power of their own words and actions. It provided the teachers with a powerful opportunity to make their collective stance on the issue known.

## Fear Prevents Presence

Figures such as 7 and 8 capture the personal issues affecting some of our youth in schools today. There are reasons why students do not attend, or cannot attend, school. We need to consider and discover what is going on in their lives outside of school that is preventing them from learning. As was the case in Figure 7, a student's negative affect or lack of attention in class may even be a cry for help. The adults in this project would never have known that this student was dealing with crippling anxiety and incredible sadness because of the gang-related murder of her cousin the night before this class period. Her drawing raised questions that prompted a conversation, ultimately resulting in counseling being offered to this student the very same day. Figure 8 poignantly reminds us that within our political landscape and the difficult struggles that families can face, the harsh realities of this life affect our students in profound ways. It is startling to realize what students hear and know about today's world, as we have become so connected. And it is sad to consider that they must take these burdens on and attempt to navigate their complexities while just trying to be kids in school. If we don't ask, we can't help.

## Teachers Should Care

All of the previous themes contain undertones of this notion: our students expect (and need) us to care. Let us not forget that care is a basic need for us all. It can certainly be a work-of-the-heart with students, but it is also a worthwhile investment in their lives and the productivity of classroom spaces. A student-centered approach to teaching and learning demands that we listen to our students and respond to their needs as we are able. Figures 12 and 20 offer examples of caring teachers who take that extra time to explain a task or to recognize and reward positive behavior. Inquiring about students' needs and interests and building learning experiences that meet these needs shows students that we care. As was the case in this project, communicating care to students changes the interactions teachers have with them. Here it created a much-needed safe place for students to share their feelings in the classroom. As Figure 11 suggests, school could be an antidote to otherwise feeling "sad." Let this inspire us!

## Other Key Findings

Beyond the student findings listed above, other unforeseen discoveries or benefits of this work also surfaced. Some students initially reported not being comfortable with the blank pieces of paper or with the free form of creative expression required for this project. They wanted us to tell them what to do or to reaffirm their work at different points along the way. However, we were very careful to remain neutral, and we did not interject more than was necessary. We felt it was important for the students to feel a bit raw and uncomfortable, but also to find their own courage and voice. Some sat for a while, some copied aspects of others' work, some laughed uncomfortably with friends before getting started. But, in time, everyone produced an artifact of their experience. Every student gave us a glimpse into his or her world.

Much to our surprise, we discovered that 6th-grade students are pretty eager to share their feelings. At the end of the class period, one student wanted to read his "bad rap"—as shown in Figure 2—out loud. Then a couple more students followed. It was amazing to witness how respectful the rest of the students were with this process. (They even clapped for each other!) But as we all know, it takes a safe and nurturing classroom environment for something like this to take place.

Related to this notion, though I barely knew these students, it was relatively easy for me to build a sense of trust with them. I was part of creating this safe space for them to share: I gave them my full attention; I was interested in what they wanted to draw or had to say; I looked and listened inquisitively and without judgment. Imagine what can be done if we show up day after day for our students in this way. These kinds of experiences form relationships with students that supersede any rule book or cool class project. I suspect that, for many students, this is where a true love for school—a spark for lifelong learning—begins. It's like we were taught in Ed Psych all those years ago: basic needs come first.

And while the student data revealed much to be considered as we attempt to understand school experiences, perhaps equally important are the takeaways the teachers reported during this project. Much to my surprise, the teachers were startled by what their students had to say. In their absolute eagerness to read each and every student's response before letting me out of the room, they realized that they didn't know some of their students as well as they thought they did. And, most important within this realization, they discovered that they needed to follow up with or even get specific help for some of their students as a result of what they learned about them.

While reacting to the pressure that they feel as public school teachers to "stay the course" and to "get through their requirements," these teachers still arrived at the notion that "they don't create enough space for these types of exercises in their class periods." Understanding the importance of creating spaces for students to share bits of themselves and their experiences in their classrooms, the teachers in this project created a plan to repeat this activity with their students once a quarter in order to do their own research of sorts: to check in more frequently (both academically and personally) with "their fragile little beings."

At the close of this project, I felt a newfound compassion emanating from these already compassionate teachers that I absolutely know will make an impact on their students' lives.

### Implications and Researcher Ruminations

These 6th-grade students have imparted many messages through their expressions, but perhaps the most important is this: middle-schoolers can be deep-thinking kiddos. It's not all Snapchat, cell phones, and outward defiance. We must not forget, in all our interactions with students, to take into consideration their complicated lives and emotional needs.

It is critical to talk to our students and to give them safe spaces to express themselves. Even on the toughest of school days, it is our duty to ask how our students are feeling and to respond with care. (This is perhaps why a day may feel so tough in the first place.) Public schools can be some of the most important spaces in which students can do this type of self-reflective work, as they may not have any other safe space available to do so. As we have witnessed here, students can be quite open and revealing in the process.

I must say that it was an honor to take part in this project with these 6th-graders. I had no idea how moved I would be during the short amount of time I spent with them; I both laughed and cried out loud. I was struck by their innocence, amused by their silliness, and saddened by some of the harsh realities of their lives. I spent hours studying some of their words and drawings, speculating about their home lives and social situations. And I rest easy in the fact that we, as educators, already know what to do to best serve our students. But as we are reminded of what we already know, we are also reminded that we are called upon to act.

I found it captivating and eye-opening to humble myself and to try to meet these students where they are—to venture underneath the surface level by digging below. Letting their stories into my heart, in fact, strengthened me as an educator. Therein lies the beauty of education. While doing work with our students, we often do work on ourselves.

## References

Bruner, J. (1991). The narrative construction of reality. *Critical Inquiry*, *18*(1), 1–21.

Clandinin, D.J., & Connelly, F.M. (2000). *Narrative inquiry: Experience and story in qualitative research*. San Francisco, CA: Jossey-Bass.

# CHAPTER SIX

# MUST WE ALWAYS STAY ON THE STRUGGLE BUS?

CHRISTOPHER BECKHAM

O NCE I TOLD A friend about a difficulty I was having teaching Plato's *Republic* to my undergraduate teacher education students. The friend remarked, "You are always on the struggle bus with that, aren't you?" I then had to struggle to find out the meaning of this expression, because I had never heard it before. As a dutiful academic, I researched the term "struggle bus" and found that it is a *neologism*. In case the term is new to my readers as well, according to the Rice University Neologisms Database, *the struggle bus* is an "an imaginary bus representing a state of perpetual struggles or difficulties" ("Struggle bus," 2013). While it may be a bit of a silly metaphor, it has a real application to the work of teaching and learning. I am convinced that any learner or teacher can profit from asking him- or herself the question, "Must we always stay on the struggle bus?"

If we are really interested in learning, I am afraid the answer is "yes." In this chapter, I argue that teachers do well to encourage students to expect to struggle to learn new and difficult content and skills. Teachers provide lasting help if they teach students to work hard and determinedly. Furthermore, I explain that when we experience the "struggle," we provide evidence that we are active in our learning. I affirm that it is active learning, not passive learning, that is vital, transformative, and lasting. Additionally, and importantly, I also want to raise a caution about overuse of rigor and challenge in the classroom. There is a need for "guardrails" to keep the "struggle bus" from veering off the road to true learning. Without care and caution, teachers who let their students struggle with "no wins" can cause them to despair. Classrooms should be places of rigor and appropriate intellectual struggle, but calls for students at any level to "accept the invitation to the pain of learning" can be misunderstood. Well-meaning efforts to encourage hard work can be overdone. My contention is that students will love, not hate, school when they are active participants in their learning, even if they have to "get on the struggle bus." However, for the struggle to pay off, students must know that their teachers are alongside them in the struggle to help and guide them when the going gets tough.

### Why Do We Need a Seat on the Struggle Bus If We Want to Learn?

For many years now, I've started my courses in teacher education with the same question: "Why do you want to be a teacher?" Responses vary, but one statement resurfaces again, and again, and again: "I want to make learning fun for my students." I appreciate the desire to lower barriers to learning, which I take to be the underlying sentiment behind the statement. However, I am dubious that they can pull it off. My preservice teacher candidates may indeed one day succeed in making their classrooms fun places; however, I have concerns about what kind of learning happens there. Learning and fun make for an odd couple, especially in the grades of middle, secondary, and post-secondary education.

I remember first confronting this notion when a colleague told me about an essay he used to open his own teacher education courses. The title of the essay is "The Invitation to the Pain of Learning," by Mortimer Adler, which appeared in 1941 in *The Journal of Educational Sociology*.[1] In this short essay, Adler, then a professor at the University of Chicago (who went on to achieve no small fame as a promoter of "The Great Books"), lamented what he called the "kindergarten spirit" that characterized much of American schooling. Arguing instead for "transformative" education, Adler insisted that students, parents, and teachers alike must accept that in education, as in all else, without some pain, there is no gain. One might acquire what he termed "factual information" from an easygoing approach, but not "genuine learning." In Adler's view, there was no way to make real, meaningful

---

1    I am in debt to my colleague Dr. Timothy L. Simpson, Morehead State University, for introducing me to Adler.

learning fun. Learning was a matter of hard work, and educators needed to be prepared to "go against the grain" when teaching students (Adler, 1990, p. 234). Adler warned that human nature was such that it preferred loafing in the classroom to toiling. He called for educators and students to steel themselves for toil and difficulty in learning. Entertainment and education had to be kept separate, and it would never do for either student or teacher to confuse and comingle the two. He never condemned entertainment; he just worried that it was making too many inroads into the classroom and with detrimental effects. As Adler put it, "anyone who has ever done any thinking, even a little bit, knows that it is painful. It is hard work—in fact the very hardest that human beings are ever called upon to do" (Adler, 1990, p. 234). If he's correct, and I think he is, then what conclusion should we draw? Namely, this: learning requires thinking, and if thinking is the hardest work we do, then learning is hard work. Adler has invited us aboard the struggle bus.

I found the essay meaningful and decided to include it in my own class reading list. For several years now, this essay is assigned right after the class when my students have pledged themselves to making their own classrooms places where "learning is fun." Engaging students with this reading is almost always a fruitful experience—lively discussions frequently occur when I ask them to think back on their own experiences as students in light of the essay. Oftentimes, as it turns out, the "fun" classes are not the ones where they themselves seem to have learned the most. Usually, they confront the fact that the classes that they had to struggle in were the ones that now mean the most to them as undergraduates.

I wondered, though, if Adler was unique in this invitation he issued. I had little exposure to his ideas in graduate school other than reading about the various controversies he and others engaged in over the literary canon. I knew nothing of his pedagogical ideas. So I set out to find out about this "pain of learning." I did not have to look far to find others who agreed. For instance, Adler's colleague and onetime president of the University of Chicago, Robert M. Hutchins, made similar points in his book *The Learning Society*. Adler and Hutchins were no small fish in the sea of educational theory. Both were voluminously published authors who commanded considerable public attention in the middle part of the 20th century. In *The Learning Society*, Hutchins warned: "In education when little is expected, little is achieved" (Hutchins, 1969, p. 27). Like Adler, Hutchins clearly espoused the "no pain, no gain" viewpoint. Hutchins expected us to have our tickets punched for the "struggle bus" if we were to learn much at all.

There is no novelty in this view. Adler and Hutchins, I discovered, were merely two members of a long procession of educators who stressed the effortful, if not toilsome, character of obtaining a genuine education. Much longer ago, none less than Aristotle, that wise ancient philosopher, remarked that "the roots of education are bitter, but the fruits are sweet."[2] This, too, seemed to be another way of saying "no pain, no gain." The quality and level of investment at the beginning of education determined the end result. If one wants to learn and learn well, then one must endure the hardships of toil and effort in the sowing and planting, if one expects to reap much in the way of a harvest. Moreover, another ancient voice, Plato, Aristotle's teacher, concurred. In Book II of *The Republic*, he has Adeimantus maintain that "nothing great is easy" (Plato, 1991, p. 42). To achieve great things requires great effort; to be greatly learned must mean it has not come easily. My list of references to support Adler was growing. Someone whose writings I had read long before Adler also sounded the same refrain. William C. Bagley, a renowned teacher educator long associated with Teachers College, Columbia University, wrote:

> The supreme lesson wrung from human experience—the lesson, namely that every advance that the world has made, every step that it has taken forward, every increment that has been added to the sum total of progress has been attained at the price of self-sacrifice and effort and struggle—at the price of doing things one does not want to do. (Bagley, 1911, p. 105)

It may not be a surprise that Bagley and Adler hold the view that active learning is a must, and that struggle in the classroom is important. Bagley was a self-professed "essentialist," and Adler has long been described as a proponent of the "perennial" philosophy.[3] However, even the father of educational Progressivism seems to say much the same thing. In *How We*

2   At least, Diogenes Laertius reported him as saying this in his *Lives and Opinions of Eminent Philosophers*.

3   For more on Bagley's essentialism, see Kandel, 1961; for more on Adler's view on the perennial philosophy, see Adler, 1951.

*Think*, John Dewey argued that it is when we struggle and are perplexed that we truly engage our faculty of reflective thinking. Apart from some difficulty, thinking does not take place. As he puts it, "thinking is not a case of spontaneous combustion; it does not occur just on general principles. There is something specific which occasions and evokes it" (Dewey, 1991, pp. 2, 12, 120). He goes on to conclude that "our progress in genuine knowledge always consists in part in the discovery of something not understood in what had previously been taken for granted as plain, obvious, matter of course" (p. 120). When we are confronted with the perplexities of life's various problems, we must build on our previously acquired meanings and see if they can help us in the struggle to acquire true understanding. This seems to be quite close to what Adler, Plato, and Bagley wrote. According to Dewey, we really learn when we encounter a perplexity and then work hard by engaging reflective thought to overcome the difficulty. If we avoid all difficulties in the classroom, we do not create the conditions for reflection to occur. Dewey thought education was a process that enabled the individual to move away from merely acting on impulses to acting intelligently and rationally through engaging in reflective thought (Dewey, 1991, p. 67). The key ingredient in "learning by doing" is coming up against a problem: something that calls forth the need for reflection. Dewey differed from the "perennial" philosophy of Adler and "essentialism" of Bagley in many significant ways, but they each agree that the *active* learner who is struggling with gaining ground in understanding is the *genuine* learner. It isn't the fun that is had that counts most in education. It is the effortful, purposeful activity of the learner that most readily results in genuine learning. Growth only occurs when challenges are presented and overcome, as Dewey so often noted in a later and equally famous book, *Experience and Education*: "... growth depends upon the presence of difficulty to be overcome by the exercise of intelligence" (Dewey, 1997, p. 79).

   Turning aside from educational philosophy, let me draw on how a specific curriculum, mathematics, uses similar language to Adler in its curricular theory. Math educators use a phrase that illustrates quite well the concept I describe: "productive struggle."[4] Hiroko K. Warshauer noted in her article

---

4   I was introduced to this concept by a Morehead State University colleague, Dr. Edna O. Schack, who pointed out to me after a presentation that Adler sounded a great deal like a math teacher calling for "productive struggle."

"Productive Struggle in Middle School Mathematics Classrooms" that it is a long accepted mathematics teaching theory that apart from students experiencing some sense of struggle in learning math, deep learning does not occur (Warshauer, 2015).

Still other terms exist for what I am using the metaphor "struggle bus" to describe. Some have used the term "intellectual virtues" (Lampert, 2001). Philip E. Dow, in *Virtuous Minds: Intellectual Character Development*, is one of them. Dow, a school superintendent and former teacher, told the story of two students confronted with reading a difficult novel for a school assignment. One student opened the book, but soon became bored and disinterested. She decided to watch a sitcom instead, and there were no pains, so to speak, involved in doing so. The sitcom entertained, but did not educate—it made no intellectual demands on her. Another student attempted the assignment and was likewise challenged at times, but nevertheless completed the task and was rewarded for her efforts through a series of enhanced learning experiences made possible only by persevering through the "pain" of learning. Dow does not suggest that the rewards of hard work in learning are immediate or even always pecuniary, but he made a strong case that one step toward intellectual indolence may eventually lead to a lifetime of bad intellectual habits. The moral of Dow's tale is that some pains now will almost always lead to a more positive outcome in the near or distant future (Dow, 2013). Buying our ticket for the struggle bus when in school helps us later in life when we continue to need to learn new and challenging lessons.

I can cite more research and writing on the value of tenacity, struggle, and the "pain of learning." Paul Tough, for example, noted the findings of Carol Dweck and Angela Duckworth and other psychological researchers in his book *How Children Succeed*. Tough noted that Duckworth and her colleagues found that "grit"—personal determination to persevere in educational settings and pursuit of long-term goals—was essential to school success (Tough, 2013). Tough reported that Dweck's findings on "growth mindsets" revealed that when students believe that intelligence is "malleable" and are praised for hard work, good things often happen in their academic performance. In other words, when students accept challenges in order to learn and grow, improvements follow. It would appear that this is a *psychological* application to Adler's more *philosophical* "invitation to the pain of learning." The literature on this subject is a burgeoning field, and one does not have to look far to find confirming data (see Garcia, 2014;

U.S. Department of Education, 2015; Kamenetz, 2015). If a student accepts the invitation to struggle and grow, and practices learning new things even if it is a painful journey, substantive learning is likely to follow. Convincing students of this is not always easy, however.

### The "Hidden Meaning" of Struggling: Creating Active Learners

As I understand the arguments of these philosophers and psychologists, they believe there are two approaches to teaching and learning. One approach is the way of active learning, and the other is the way of passive learning. These advocates for struggle, hard work, and effort all seem to make the same call for active learning. Active, not passive, learning is a must, and active learning requires persistence, perseverance, and a willingness to engage with challenging material. As Dewey explained, genuine education is not a matter of a teacher dictating material to students, which would be a fair way to describe "passive learning," but rather, education should be a "co-operative enterprise." Gains are made in learning when there is "reciprocal give-and-take" (Dewey, 1977, p. 72). Students must be active participants in the acquisition of knowledge, not passive sponges memorizing facts.

It is hard to find the word "fun" in these descriptions, but a more complete picture is needed. What does "active learning" look like? How can we tell when a teacher, for example, values active learning as opposed to passive learning? Adler insisted that active vs. passive learning occurred when teaching led students through a "process of discovery, in which the student is the main agent, not the teacher," and when it "involves the mind, not just the memory" (Adler, 1982, p. 50; Adler, 1990, p. 168).

More recent studies offer similar insights. In 2004, a study entitled "Inside the Classroom" was conducted by Iris R. Weiss, Joan D. Pasley, and colleagues. They reported their findings in an article for *Educational Leadership* and explained that classrooms featuring active learners rated highest in their study. Their article, entitled "What Is High-Quality Instruction?" noted that classrooms where teachers managed to combine "rigor" and "respect for students" best met the criteria for high-quality instruction. They noted that it was inherently difficult for teachers to combine these two things, but through the use of effective questioning and providing "clear explanations at appropriate junctures," teachers could succeed in providing high-quality, engaging instruction. They noted that effective teaching goes far beyond mere "telling"—whereby the student is doing little more than "sit and get." On the contrary, student engagement through active learn-ing—where the teachers asked lots of thought-inducing questions—was a critical ingredient in high-quality instruction (Weiss & Pasley, 2004). Active student participation, in Weiss and Pasley's view, meant that students were challenged by their teachers' use of engaging questions. The students were then expected to respond in developmentally appropriate ways. Classrooms that feature active learning by students are not classrooms where "fill in the blank questions in rapid-fire fashion" predominate (Weiss & Pasley, 2004, p. 27). Rather, students are asked questions that require them to think deeply about the content.

## A Necessary Caution

As I mentioned in the introduction to this chapter, though, there is some danger in this call to build persistence and perseverance through active learning and struggle in the classroom. In my own teaching of undergradu-ate teacher education students, I have seen how balance and care are needed when discussing the "invitation to the pain of learning."

Adler's essay must be a jarring piece of writing for my students, because they tend to remember it throughout the semester. However, they sometimes misunderstand Adler's point. They equate "the pain of learning" with an ability to endure boredom and the exactions of drill and discipline in the classroom. The "pain of learning," in their minds, becomes a matter of sore-ness from sitting still too long or having to do too much homework at night. It takes careful explanation to show them that the hard work that Adler and all these others are calling for does not merely mean building one's capac-ity to listen to really long lectures. They mistakenly assume that Adler and others who advocate rigor must be an advocate of "sit and get" and "drill and kill" teaching strategies. Adler advocated nothing of the kind (Adler, 1982, pp. 49–56). I therefore often remind my teacher education students that teaching with precision and rigor does not mean that one must con-stantly lecture. I have to work hard to avoid creating the impression with my students that "the pain of learning" is just one more awful experience on the way to adulthood, akin to receiving one's vaccinations or swallowing some awful-tasting medicine in order to get well. I do not think that is what Adler, Bagley, and company meant, even though sometimes my students mistakenly conclude this. These theorists wanted readers to understand that students had to be active participants if they really wanted to learn things that mattered, things that could change their lives for the better. Perhaps one more quote from Adler can clarify just what he meant:

> [U]nless we acknowledge that every invitation to learning can promise pleasure only as the result of pain, can offer achievement only at the expense of work, all of our invitations to learning, in school and out...will be as much buncombe as the worst patent medicine advertising, or the campaign pledge to put two chickens in every pot. (Adler, 1990, p. 236)

In addition, while William C. Bagley strongly advocated the need to let students "struggle" in order to learn, he did not countenance the view that this meant that teachers should be obtuse or purposely set impossible obstacles in their students' paths. Encouraging growth through hard work did not equate with calling on students to achieve perfection or perform tasks that were far beyond their developmental abilities. As he stated, "While I insist strenuously that the most useful lesson we can teach our pupils is how to do disagreeable tasks cheerfully and willingly, please do not understand me to mean that we should go out of our way to provide disagreeable tasks" (Bagley, 1911, pp. 103–104).

Bagley recalled that he knew a teacher who went "out of his way" to make learning unpleasant for his students by creating "distasteful tasks" for them in an ill-conceived attempt to build what he called "patience and persistence." The teacher in question would not assist students in any way, and did not develop careful lessons in the shaky belief that this forced the students to do more of their own work. Bagley was not impressed.

> The great trouble with this teacher is that his policy does not work out in practice. A small minority of his pupils are strengthened by it; the majority are weakened...a pupil gains no strength out of obstacles that he fails to overcome...when defeat follows defeat and failure follows failure, it is weakness that is being engendered— not strength. And that is the trouble with this teacher's pupils. The majority leave him with all confidence in their own ability shaken out of them and some of them never recover from the experience. (Bagley, 1911, p. 103)

### Inspiration for Teachers Who Want to Buy Their Ticket for "the Struggle Bus" and Invite Students Along for the Ride

If my readers grant that I am correct on this one point—namely, that getting on the "struggle bus" is a necessary condition for genuine learning—then they probably wish to raise a question. What, then, do I see as the role of teachers after the invitation to students is made? Am I calling for teachers to be cruel taskmasters, charging their students to make bricks without straw? Do I want teachers to adopt a "sink or swim, kid" attitude? (Tough, 2013, pp. 97–98). No; the opposite is true. If teachers decide that the way of effort and grit is the best take on teaching and learning, then they must redouble their efforts to be excellent, inspiring teachers who know just when and how to encourage students in their struggles to learn.

Recently, *Education Week* conducted an interview of three math teachers, asking them about the challenges of their work. One of them, Makeda Brome, gave this particularly insightful comment about the nature of her work as a math teacher where struggle is concerned: "Our subject is about productive struggle, solving everyday problems, and seeing patterns in the world around us. Challenges are a natural part of mathematics. As teachers, we have to make it our goal to overcome classroom challenges so that our students learn" (Ferlazzo, 2017). Brome's point here seems to be that if math teachers call on their students to engage in productive struggle in order to succeed at math, then math teachers must accept the reality of productive struggle in their work as teachers. Teachers must constantly struggle themselves in the quest to learn how to teach better, more effectively, and with high quality. It is never just the student who needs a ticket for the struggle bus. For those familiar with Platonic dialogues that feature Socrates, it seems that this was exactly the case with Socrates. Again and again, Socrates expresses doubts about ideas and positions being taken, modelling before students the kind of intellectual struggle that good teaching and genuine learning require. Good teaching does not happen apart from rigorous application any more than genuine learning can. Where, then, might we look for examples of "just when and how" to encourage students either to accept "the invitation to the pain of learning" in the first place or how to persevere when the invitation is accepted and the going gets rough?

In the first place, we have to be up front with our students that "the struggle is going to be real," as they might say. Teachers must put the cards on the table, so to speak, and early on, that real learning only happens through hard work. H.K. Warshauer's work, which I referenced above, is instructive on this point. Warshauer argued that frankly acknowledging that "doing math" almost always requires struggle is an important first step. In other words, teachers need to prepare their students by letting them know that it is normal to experience difficulty and that the teacher is there to help, but not do the work for them. She found that when teachers, through deliberate statements and actions, explained that struggle is natural, and that they were there to guide and help, their students handled it better. They knew it was coming and that it was typical. I believe that what she says about mathematics is true for any discipline—indeed, it is true for all of genuine education. If teachers communicate that learning, *real learning*, always requires a level of effort and application that is strenuous, students benefit. In other words, as teachers, our goal is not to be agents of fun in the classroom; rather, it is to be friendly conductors doubling as fellow passengers on the "struggle bus." As teachers work hard to learn, students can be inspired to do the same. As Warshauer so well explained, classroom culture goes a long way toward building the capacity of students to engage in productive struggle (Warshauer, 2015, pp. 393–394).

In my own work in teacher education, I have tried a variety of approaches to show teachers-in-training that they must have high expectations for their students, and themselves, in regard to their learning. As I ask much of them in their undergraduate class, I remind them that one day they will ask much of their own students. If they accept "the invitation to the pain of learning" as undergraduates, they will not regret it—rather, they will be better teachers for it. It is incumbent on me, however, to show them how teachers who call for active learning "do" their work.

Adler's essay is not the only arrow in my quiver when trying to get this idea across. A classic text in the literature of teaching and learning provides similar encouragement by way of a completely different genre. Jesse Stuart's semi-autobiographical *The Thread That Runs So True* recounts his own trials and travails as a student and a teacher in early 20th-century Appalachia. Stuart struggled mightily to better himself through education—and struggle really is the important word there. Having once gained enough schooling to become a credentialed teacher, though, he did not stop learning. The struggle to learn was lifelong for him. I have found it to be an excellent resource to reinforce the points that Adler, Dewey, and others have made, but from a different angle and different sort of reading material. Stuart's language and cadences are familiar to many of my students. One commented that Stuart reminded him of his grandfather, a retired teacher. Stuart's calls for active learning and engaged teaching are subtler than Adler, Bagley, and even Dewey, but he still makes the same point.

Time and again, Stuart urged his students to accept that toil was not wasted when applied to learning. In one particularly poignant vignette, Stuart described how one high school mathematics teaching experience taught him "just when and how to encourage" his own students in their struggles. He was teaching at "Winston High School," a small school in a rural village in Eastern Kentucky, and a student came to him needing help with an algebra problem. Stuart wrote: "I looked at the problem. It was a problem about trains starting at given points and running toward each other so many miles per hour and how long would it be before they met. I had never solved this problem in my first year algebra" (Stuart, 1949, p. 76).

He told his student that he could not work the problem. The student replied: "Mr. Stuart, I understand. You want your pupils to work these problems, don't you?" Stuart had been honest, but the question was a good one. He replied, "Yes, if they can." The student took the challenge, and worked on the problem for about 30 minutes. Returning to Stuart's desk, the student showed him the answer, and he was able to trace back through the steps and conclude that the student was indeed correct. The students did not know that many times the teacher was only slightly more knowledgeable than they were as they worked through their algebra problems the rest of the year. They tackled the problems with enthusiasm and worked together (Stuart, 1949, p. 77).

Stuart reflected on this experience for the benefit of his readers. He considered how his encouragement and willingness to let the student struggle with the problem on his own, so long as the student knew he could ask for help, made for active learning. He said this experience and others like it, as they worked through their algebra and plane geometry lessons, gave him increased sympathy for his students' struggle and empathy for the contextual factors that affected them. He ultimately concluded that when he had to struggle to teach difficult concepts clearly, he taught better. He deduced that the students learned better as a result. Time and again in his work as an educator, Stuart, through observation, found that by coming alongside students in the struggle to learn, happy results followed. I believe that pointing out these lessons as we read the material together helps my own teacher education students.

Later in his career, while teaching remedial English at "Dartmouth High School," Stuart inquired what his students' main difficulties in learning High School English had been. For many of them, it was Shakespeare. He was sympathetic. Even though he was an accomplished teacher and a widely published author by this point, he had struggled to learn Shakespeare in high school. He told his students this. They felt better about themselves when they realized Shakespeare had also been difficult for their teacher. However, he did not excuse them from the work. He flatly told them that they must accept the struggle ahead and learn to master English if they wanted to get ahead in the world (Stuart, 1949, p. 271). To help with this, Stuart used both traditional and non-traditional methods alike with his students—from memorization of poetry to diagramming sentences to reading student-composed themes. He won their trust by honestly pointing out his own struggles to learn what he asked them to learn. As Stuart put it, "with this group I worked, laughed, and talked. I tried to be a stabilizing influence. I tried to let them take responsibility. They accepted responsibility. They loved it too" (p. 277). The students loved learning not because it was easy for them, but because they accepted the struggles and knew their teacher was alongside them in the work. Another English teacher, Richard Mitchell, made a similar point in *The Gift of Fire*. As he put it, "while no one else can nourish me, I will never be nourished by those who are not themselves nourished, never brought into thoughtfulness unless others have gone there before me" (Mitchell, 1987, ¶35).

As one reads through the pages of *The Thread That Runs So True*, one "thread" is woven through the entire tale: as a teacher, he was there to guide, to help—and, of course, to instruct. He could not do one thing for his students, though. He could not learn for them and he could not take the struggle out of learning for them. In rural and urban settings alike, Stuart consistently taught his students that hard work was just part of what it meant to be a student—and that their own efforts in learning were irreplaceable. Ambition and a concerted effort on the part of the student were key. When both Stuart and his students accepted their seats on the "struggle bus," so to speak, academic, social, emotional, and intellectual flourishing followed. *The Thread That Runs So True* is a moving story of what can happen when student and teacher alike accept the maxim given by Aristotle so long ago.

## Conclusion

I began this chapter with a question: "Must we always remain on the struggle bus?" Although I am using a possibly silly idiom, it seems to me a question well worth pondering. I think the answer we provide is what determines the outcome we will experience. If as teachers we climb aboard the "struggle bus," convince our students to join us, and struggle to learn new things, we likely will do just that—learn new things. If we want a quality, transformative, or to use Adler's word "genuine" education and we say "Yes! Let me on the struggle bus!" then we will likely look at the results we achieve with happiness. Progress comes only through grappling with the unfamiliar, which can be daunting. If we say no, we may have an easier time of things in the classroom and elsewhere, but to what ultimate advantage?

The cost of a true education is high. It comes at the cost of a lifelong struggle and a lifelong willingness to accept "the invitation to the pain of learning." However, as Aristotle, Jesse Stuart, and others along with him have noted, the dividends are rich, and well worth it. As Stuart explained: "Education [is] not a commodity to be bought and sold but something that [gives] one more realization and enjoyment of the many things that life held in store… with more education, the mysteries and beauties of life would unfold before them like the buds of leaf and flower in the spring" (Stuart, 1949, p. 180).

I think students will love learning and yes, perhaps even love school if it is a place of academic challenge, yet a place where they know the teachers will support them, and a place where teachers are honest and upfront with students that apart from taking some pains with learning, there will be no substantial gains. It is true; *I am always on the struggle bus*, as my friend said. However, I think the destination is worth it.

## References

Adler, M.J. (1951, October 1). Labor, leisure and liberal education. *Journal of General Education*, 6(11), 35–45.

Adler, M.J. (1982). *The paideia proposal*. New York: Macmillan.

Adler, M.J. (1990). *Reforming education: The opening of the American mind* (G. Van Doren, Ed.). New York: Collier Books.

Bagley, W.C. (1911). *Craftsmanship in teaching*. New York: Macmillan.

Dewey, J. (1991). *How we think*. New York: Prometheus Books.

Dewey, J. (1997). *Experience and education*. New York: Touchstone.

Dow, P.E. (2013). *Virtuous minds: Intellectual character development*. Downers Grove, IL: InterVarsity Press.

Ferlazzo, L. (2017, February 11). Response: "Challenges are a natural part of mathematics." Classroom Q&A with Larry Ferlazzo Blog, *Education Week*. http://blogs.edweek.org/teachers/classroom_qa_with_larry_ferlazzo/2017/02/response_challenges_are_a_natural_part_of_mathematics.html

Garcia, E. (2014, December 2). *The need to address noncognitive skills in the education policy agenda*. Economic Policy Institute, Briefing Paper #386. http://www.epi.org/publication/the-need-to-address-noncognitive-skills-in-the-education-policy-agenda/

Hutchins, R. M. (1969). *The learning society*. New York: Mentor.

Kamenetz, A. (2015, May 28). Nonacademic skills are key to success. But what should we call them? Retrieved February 9, 2017, from http://www.npr.org/sections/ed/2015/05/28/404684712/non-academic-skills-are-key-to-success-but-what-should-we-call-them

Kandel, I.L. (1961). *William Chandler Bagley: Stalwart educator*. New York: Bureau of Publications.

Plato. (1991). *The Republic of Plato* (A. Bloom, Trans.) (2nd ed.). New York: Basic Books.

Lampert, M. (2001). *Teaching problems and the problems of teaching*. New Haven, CT: Yale University Press.

Mitchell, R. (1987). *The gift of fire*. New York: Simon and Schuster. http://www.sourcetext.com/grammarian/gift-of-fire/index.html

"Struggle bus." (2013). *The Rice University Neologisms Database*. Accessed August 25, 2017. http://neologisms.rice.edu/index.php?a=term&d=1&t=18165

Stuart, J. (1949). *The thread that runs so true*. New York: Charles Scribner's Sons.

Tough, P. (2013). *How children succeed: Grit, curiosity, and the hidden power of character*. New York: Mariner Books.

U.S. Department of Education. (2015, March 10). *Non-cognitive factors session*. White Paper by Suchi Saxena. https://www.charterschoolcenter .org/sites/default/files/files/field_publication_attachment/Non-Cognitive%20Factors_0.pdf

Warshauer, H.K. (2015). Productive struggle in middle school mathematics classrooms. *Journal of Math Teacher Education, 18*(4), 375–400.

Weiss, I.R., & Pasley, J.D. (2004, February). Inside the classroom. *Educational Leadership, 61*(5), 24–27.

# CHAPTER SEVEN

# ICELANDIC EDUCATION AT HATEIGSSKOLI

## Giving Students Wings

KARLA SMART-MORSTAD AND SARA TRIGGS

IN AN EARLIER PUBLICATION entitled *Why Kids Hate School* (2007), we questioned whether or not some children might hate school because their potential is limited by curricular mandates and the instructional parameters of teachers.

> Maybe kids "hate" school because their potential is often dismissed. This can happen when standardized test scores indicating students' success are valued over a clear understanding of the breadth and depth of *what more* children can achieve. If legislative mandates for curriculum and instruction rested on the understanding of the philosophical nature of potential, then maybe education could be different enough to recognize and expand students' potential. (Smart & Triggs, 2007, p. 97)

In our travels we found a school where we believe the philosophical nature of potential is applied to students' education and where students are provided with opportunities to strive toward reaching individual potential through engagement, discovery, creation, and sense of being. What we found was a school where students' voices and ideas are acknowledged and applied to decisions in the school. Where curriculum was broad and engaging to sustain students' interests and address more than just their academic needs. Where, if an individual did not have a love of math to draw them to school, perhaps art, drama, dance, woodshop, or textiles would provide the needed incentive to hold students' interest and keep them involved. Where thinking and reflection are valued as legitimate endeavors, and students are afforded the time to do so. Where school and curriculum provide for understanding of self, communication, culture, and others. Where critical thinking, creativity, and risk taking are valued over uniformity. Where what is valued as a community is reflected in its motto, "Respect—Cooperation—Happiness." Where we found this place was at Hateigsskoli (How-tegs-skol-lee) School in Reykjavik, Iceland. Drawn to the dynamics of the school environment, we returned four times—in 2010, 2011, 2013, and 2016. Our research there included interviews, observation, participant observation, and reflection on what we saw and experienced with students, teachers, administrators, and parents.

## The Country of Iceland

The nation of Iceland, near the Arctic Circle, is a geologically young island formed of lava rock. Moss grows heartily, but trees are scarce. Settled by Norwegian Vikings and the Irish women they captured to bring with them, Iceland remains relatively homogeneous. Home to the world's first parliament, which met at Thingvellir in the year 930, Iceland today is governed by Social Democrats in a coalition of center and left political parties. Like the United States, Iceland experienced an economic crash in 2008. Unlike in the United States, the Icelandic government voted to allow defaulting banks to fail. The economic crash, or "the crisis," as we heard many Icelanders refer to it, is steadily improving, but remains a source of pain for the government, private and public companies, and families. The psychological damage experienced by families during this time continues to affect the health of students in the schools today. A more recent disruption in the Icelandic government was the April 2016 release of the Panama Papers, which disclosed illegal offshore financial holdings of the prime minister and led to his resignation. While destroying the nation's trust in government officials, it brings the promise of new elections in the fall.

Fishing, aluminum smelting, geothermal energy, sheep and wool production, and export of Icelandic horses, from Viking stock, fuel the economy. The most dramatic change in the country's industry is tied to the massive influx of international tourists over the past three years. The number of tourists in Iceland jumped from 400,000 yearly to nearly a million and a half. Active volcanoes, geysers, geothermal pools, waterfalls, black sand lava beaches, hiking, and whale watching bring a global audience to Iceland. The impact of this is visible as you walk through Reykjavik. The city is alive with work on infrastructure. We counted at least ten multistory cranes in the five-block radius of our hotel. Iceland, which has typically limited the number of immigrants entering the country, is asking itself how it will meet the demands of the tourist industry without opening its borders.

Meeting with many Icelanders on our visits, we found an unquestionable value of creativity. Asgeir Beinteinsson, principal of the school we visit, explains how Icelanders differ from other Scandinavians: "Of the Nordic countries, Iceland is more like America in valuing individualism over community and not standing out. There is a Nordic belief that everybody should be equal and no one should be more excellent than the next one," he tells us. Then, in a Nordic way, Asgeir continues, "Creativity is a deep part of the culture. I'm trying not to boast, but Iceland, with 300,000 souls, has had a global impact for creativity. Everyone knows Bjork. There are international music festivals here in Iceland; we have actors in drama in London on the stage." As an explanation, he offers this: "There must be something we are doing. Maybe it is because we are so few that each individual has enough space to make a difference."

Not long ago, Asgeir and members of his staff visited the Ardley Green Junior School of London in the United Kingdom. During a return visit to Hateigsskoli, educators from Ardley Green told Asgeir that, while schools in England give students roots, Icelandic schools give them wings. "School is not only about classical academics; it's also about extra curriculum that can prepare these students for life," he explains. Using a metaphor of a forest to describe the human mind, Asgeir says, "Creative things keep the mind aired. The trees are the academics—the creative winds need to blow through the trees."

## The City of Reykjavik

The coastal city of Reykjavik is the capital of Iceland. Known as the City of Peace, the population of 125,000 exists with no armed police force. The Cold War ended in Reykjavik where, in 1986, Gorbachev and Reagan shook hands, representing the end of what the city's former mayor refers to as the "grotesque arms race between the superpowers" (Gnarr, 2014, p. 140). Modeling the intense commitment to creativity, as well as peace, Reykjavik is a member of the International Cities of Refuge Network and "offers politically persecuted writers and poets asylum, shelter, and protected space for their writing" (Gnarr, 2014, pp. 140–141). When the U.S. air space closed on September 11, 2001, many inbound international flights to the east coast were rerouted to Iceland. In a show of compassion, all passengers were housed in the city of Reykjavik until flights were rerouted. These, in addition to numerous other events, indicate that Reykjavik, the City of Peace, has earned that label.

## Hateigsskoli School

The atmosphere at Hateigsskoli is welcoming—homelike in many ways. Students refer to faculty and administration by their first names, an approach to democracy found in schools across Scandinavia. When we arrive, children's work is seen everywhere: from the red spring tulips and yellow daffodil projects visible through a classroom window to the transparent works of art that create a stained-glass appearance across the length of the school entrance. Little feet carrying big backpacks climb the seven steps to the school's entrance, where footwear is removed. In the entryway, racks of colorful shoes and boots, arranged by grade level, await their owners at the end of the school day. When the building was new, children removed their shoes to protect the flooring and keep the building clean. But it did not take long to realize that, with students in stocking feet, the school was quieter and kids could more easily pull their feet up to sit comfortably if they chose. While some teachers and staff wear shoes, others, including Asgeir, change into clogs for the school day. Plastic shoes are available in every classroom in case of fire emergency.

Hateigsskoli, a neighborhood 1st- to 10th-grade public school, serves 440 students. Principal Asgeir Beinteinsson studied philosophy and teacher education at the University of Iceland. "I was always interested in the why of teaching," he tells us. "The best thing is to be in education—to be a part of changing society for the better." Asgeir served Hateigsskoli as vice-principal from 1991 through 1996, becoming principal in 1997. An aim of the school is that "education should be carried out in a warm and creative environment where everyone is shown respect as an individual."[1] Hateigsskoli is organized into three levels. The 1st through 4th grades (the primary grades) focus on fundamentals. The intermediate grades, 5th through 7th, identify critical thinking as a priority, and 8th through 10th grades are subject-and discipline-focused, with one-fourth of students' courses being chosen electives. Graduation takes place following the 10th grade, and students who elect to continue their education enroll in pre-university schooling or trades education.

Throughout all grade levels, about 50% of the classes are what American schools would consider academically focused, while the remaining 50% are spent in curricular areas meant to develop the potential of the whole child. Children's days are filled with art, textiles, home economics, woodshop, dance, drama, religion, physical education, and life skills.

A listed aim of the school is that "every teacher should consider all the students as their own."[2] Asgeir tells us, "Everyone at the school should be involved with all of the children in guiding, encouraging, and praising." A hallmark characteristic we see at Hateigsskoli, one that supports it as a school where students want to be, is a high sense of trust. Asgeir trusts teachers, and, as our observations show, teachers trust students. "I want everyone to blossom. I want freedom for teachers to teach to the best of their abilities," Asgeir explains. "Some teaching practices I like better than others, particularly the ones with more diversity in their style, but more traditional teachers can get the same results, and that's okay with me." Asgeir's approach gives the teachers full responsibility in their teaching and recognizes that there is more than one route to the final goal. Results are seen when the school motto, "Respect—Cooperation—Happiness," is realized through creative, critical learning. "Only when the results break down do I become concerned or involved. If the kids aren't happy, or if there are problems within the classroom between the kids, or if the learning isn't taking shape and our evaluation shows it," Asgeir tells us, "then I become concerned."

We see the school's motto come to life at the school sing-along. Every Friday morning begins with Asgeir and Hulda Gudjonsdottir, the school's evaluation director, hosting a school sing-along. With Hulda at the piano and Asgeir in the lead, the students sing familiar Icelandic folk and camp songs, complete with gestures. First- through 10th-graders sit in community on the floor of the multi-purpose auditorium, which also serves as a dance studio, lunchroom, and performance hall. Songs are largely known by heart, but the lyrics are projected on a large screen visible to all. Asgeir tells us that this enhances the reading skills of all students, especially 1st-graders who sit in the front row. Sometimes musicians from Reykjavik, or parent volunteers, join and play their instruments. There is a sense of joy in the singing that is unlike what we are familiar with from our structured experiences in choir. We are surprised to see the older children actively participating—for example, two 7th-grade girls comfortable enough to immerse themselves in the silly actions that accompany some songs. A few teachers at the entryway can be seen singing and swaying to the music, as Asgeir directs them all with grand gestures. We describe the mood with two words: community and happy.

The value of community is additionally seen for adults as well as children during morning break. While children have their morning snack, supervised by teacher aides, teachers meet in the staff room for morning coffee. A light breakfast is served, and faculty gather with Asgeir for 20 minutes of social conversation, mind-teaser games, or quick conferences. It is interesting to see time set aside for the teachers to simply socially interact with no particular agenda. We can sense the atmosphere of connectedness among the faculty and Asgeir during this time.

## Curriculum at Hateigsskoli

Icelandic educational reform in 2013 brought students' abilities, rather than their store of knowledge, to the forefront of assessment. At the same time, Iceland mandated six concepts or themes to be included in all courses at all grade levels. As Asgeir tells us, "The themes are to become an integral part of all the subject areas, but no one tells us how to do this." The six strands name values held by Icelanders. Equality, sustainability, creativity, literacy, democracy and human rights, and health and welfare are concepts educators weave into their courses and students encounter throughout their education. Meeting the challenge is sometimes frustrating, Asgeir reports. But we are energized by the results we see and hear about while at the school.

The curriculum at Hateigsskoli is ripe with opportunities that may not be considered essential by all educators, but that certainly evoke interest, creativity, and motivation on the part of the students. In addition to academic subjects, requirements include woodshop, textiles, art, drama, dance, home economics, physical education, swimming, religion, and music. What interested us was not only the incredible variety in students' school days at Hateigsskoli, but also the freedom provided within subject areas and learning activities. We observed children with time and opportunity to think, wonder, and problem-solve. We observed a school purposeful in valuing creativity, listening to students' voices, developing a sense of individuality, and building community, safety, and security. The classes that most captured our interests, and that we chose to focus on, were textiles, woodshop, and drama. In these curricular areas we saw the most student engagement, freedom, creativity, critical thinking, and problem-solving.

### Textiles and Woodshop

The environment in the textile and woodshop classes drew us in. Neither is a curriculum area we are accustomed to seeing in an elementary setting. The 4th grade marks the beginning of children's experiences in these two classes. Art, textiles, and woodshop teachers collaborate on a project that combines each discipline to develop a truly integrative experience for students' creativity and critical thinking. The experience centers on a teddy bear. In textiles, the students sew a teddy bear and knit a wardrobe for it. In woodshop, the children make a bed for the bear, and in art they create an accordion-fold picture book for the bear to teach it letters and simple words. While much of this activity, technically speaking, seems like more than a 10-year-old would be able to master, the technical skills learned (sewing, knitting, sawing, and measuring) are only the beginning of the learning that occurs. As American educators hearing of the project, we envisioned 24 uniform bears, in matching clothes with matching patterns, and a standard wooden bed. We could not have been more wrong. In addition to learning to sew, measure, saw, nail, glue, and paint, the students were invited to create. There was not a single pattern for them to use to make the bear; instead, they each designed their own. Through some samples, and trial and error, students developed the concept of moving a design from two-dimensional fabric to a three-dimensional bear. This real-life exploration, with a personalized product that they valued, helped children to understand that the pattern they thought was perfect changed as an additional dimension was added. Students learned to adapt their patterns, taking this new understanding into consideration.

Another skill taught in 4th-grade textiles for this project was knitting. Again we had envisioned a universal pattern for the teddy bears' knitted clothing; however, as each bear was an individual's creation, there was not a single pattern that would apply to all. Once more the students were left to apply what they had learned about the process of knitting to create clothing appropriate for their new friend. The pants, scarves, and hats varied in size, color, and design. Also unique to each child's design was the drawstring bag, sewn and embroidered with the bear's name, made for carrying the bear home.

While they were knitting in textiles, students were designing beds for their bears in woodshop. Our visions of a cookie-cutter pattern were dashed when we saw the variety of creations set before us. Not only did the cradles vary in color and embellishment, but each child designed his or her own headboard and footboard pattern for the bed. We saw a bed with a heart-shaped headboard, one with a teddy bear's initial cutout on top, and one shaped like a skull and crossbones. In a process that could have more easily led to multiple uniform products, children were provided the opportunity to make their learning their own. All learned the skills required for the class-work and did so in their own unique way.

Children continue on in textiles after this initial 4th-grade experience. Once they learn basic skills, they are able to think about what they might want or need and then design a project to create it. Observing a 10th-grade classroom, we notice a variety of projects going on at the same time. Two students are making slippers out of sheep's wool; a boy is completing a drawstring sack he designed to hold his Rubik's Cube; and still others are knitting hats. We observe two boys folding origami paper cranes, which does not seem related to the class. The textile teacher, Gudny Einarsdottir, explains that the students are trying to think of an idea to pursue next. She encourages them to spend time processing. "If you need time to think, then paint or fold origami to get your creativity moving," she tells students. It is not the number of finished projects that interest her; rather, it is the thinking and processing that go on in students' planning and execution. "Everyone does not have to finish at the same time. They think and work at their own speed. I am happy with one or two projects. I give them time to think, write about it, use math," she tells us. "I tell students to think of what you want to make, make a model, try it. Can it be made in textiles?"

Gudny's teaching integrates the concept of sustainability into the textile classroom. "I teach them to 'use what you have, buy nothing,'" she explains.

Gudny shows us several examples of pillows made from old T-shirts and pants. We even notice a bucket of mismatched socks at the front of the room and imagine what they may one day become. Gudny models sustainability to the class through her own choices, wearing repurposed clothing. Her dress is made from a blouse lengthened to become a shirt-dress. A row of decorative buttons marks the space where the additional fabric attaches to the dress. Gudny wants students to reuse and repurpose what they have around them. Protecting the environment and teaching students to think like planetary protectors is part of the sustainability value each subject matter is to address in the Icelandic curriculum. But Gudny knows that teaching students to make stuffed animals, or to knit caps, or to sew pajamas from what is readily available, means materials will likely be on hand at home.

Visiting the woodshop, we sense a similar valuing of problem-solving, freedom, and creativity. Again, multiple projects are occurring throughout the room as Frida Agnarsdottir, the woodshop teacher, circles the room addressing questions as they arise. One boy uses a hammer and chisel to carve out the center of a boat. Several others cut wood pieces into their desired shapes using electric saws, and another is finishing a wooden model of an antique car. We observe one young boy who seems intently focused on his work. We ask about his project, and he indicates that he is making what he calls a lock box. Through discussion we learn that this was not a project introduced by his teacher, but instead something he saw on the internet. He shows us how pieces fit together; a string will be used to pull up a handle that will open two small compartments. The intricacy of the work amazes us. We cannot understand how all of these movable pieces will be put together and work. Interviewing the shop teacher, we ask about the project. She shrugs her shoulders and chuckles. "I don't even understand how he is doing it," Frida indicates. We are impressed with her willingness to let him fly, reaching out into something she herself is unfamiliar with. We thought of the profound impact this environment of risk taking, both on the part of the teacher and the student, holds. We were witnessing trust, creativity, skill, critical thinking, and perseverance.

**Drama**

Drama is a curriculum requirement at Hateigsskoli. This is not surprising, given that one of the aims listed on the school website is "Education should encourage initiative, imagination and the courage to perform."[3] Much like in textiles and woodshop, the craft of theater is used to stretch students in many directions. It integrates other academics and provides ample opportunity for creativity. Since 2011, the Icelandic National Curriculum has required schools to include either theater or dance. Prior to this mandate, Hateigsskoli offered both and continues to do so. At Hateigsskoli, drama begins with 5th-graders. "In 1st through 4th grade," Asgeir explains, "the question is 'What is a still image?' Then, 5th- through 7th-graders study drama, while 8th- through 10th-grade students may select drama as an elective."

Asgeir and his faculty value the opportunities inherent in theater experience. "Drama is about discipline and self-control. You learn to be part of a group and you have to be silent. The crowd, including younger students, is watching intensely. There are certain rules. [You must] be quiet, listen, look, and say thank you," Asgeir tells us. While part of drama is simply fun, learning through theater is a discipline. The discipline asks much of students. Asgeir articulates what learning in theater requires: "They must learn working with others; being creative; being willing to be creative in a safe and good environment where no one laughs at you; self-discipline, for example, no talking backstage; respect for the actors on the stage; working in groups; creating respect for peers at all grades; and self-confidence. And, we see that drama teaches vocabulary."

While we are at Hateigsskoli, 5th-graders present their theater production to parents. Before the afternoon production, in textiles class, the teacher helps a wolf with the fastenings on the wooly costume he made for himself. In the theater class, the teacher emphasizes vocabulary included in the play, linking it to history and to literature. The presentation itself begins with group singing and a parent volunteer playing the saxophone. The play, based on a familiar Icelandic saga storyline, is written by students. The audience includes parents and invited guests who have often worked creatively with the students in music and filmmaking at the school. "The production was applauded by the older students in its initial presentation [earlier in the day]," Asgeir tells us. Now it receives compliments from adults.

"In drama, you are working in a group. If they feel safe in drama with peers, the children bully less. The 5th-graders receive accolades and praise from upper-grade students for their drama production," Asgeir says. The recognition given to their creativity strengthens students' relationships throughout the school. One aspect of the worthiness of drama, as Asgeir explains, is that "it makes other disciplines better." In 2003, a grant from the Icelandic Ministry of Education funded teachers to learn how to use the methods of drama in history and literature classes. "Iceland is the first country, other than Australia, to introduce drama into the national curriculum," Asgeir reflects.

## Unique Learning Projects

In addition to its rich and engaging curriculum, Hateigsskoli features special learning events that occur throughout the school year. "Our school has been known for being receptive to new ideas," Asgeir tells us. This is evident in the unique learning projects they have integrated into their school year. Some ideas were suggested by outsiders; some were adapted, expanded, and improved; and others evolved from student suggestions. The Cultural Encounter, Carousel, Hilmar Film Festival, and Multiple Intelligence Days are four such events. The rationales for the activities vary, but all actively involve students in further understanding themselves, their relationships to others, communication, and community.

### The Cultural Encounter

An example of the school's valuing of individual exploration, understanding of others, and creativity is their active engagement with the Cultural Encounter School Network. Hateigsskoli was the first school in Iceland to try the Cultural Encounter model in 2008, when Danish educator Kristin Vilhjalmsdottir brought the idea to Asgeir. As members of a participating school, Hateigsskoli's 5th-graders are engaged in an extended learning project known as the Cultural Encounter. The project asks for self-expression and information about a topic or pursuit. "Although we are all part of a culture, with each and every individual, we have our own personal culture," Asgeir explains.

Kristin Vilhjalmsdottir shared a website[4] describing the Cultural Encounter, from which we learn that "students, parents, and staff members get an opportunity to introduce their culture and interests in a fun and lively way within an encouraging environment." The website states the goals of the project, including "that people of all origin living in Iceland should feel proud of their own culture and share those feelings with others, to evolve children's ability to be active members in society and for them to realize the fact that different cultures can enrich their own, support a respectful integration, and stimulate the children's fantasy, curiosity and creativity."

We see the Cultural Encounter as a particularly beneficial endeavor. It not only allows students to see that they, as well as their knowledge and interests, are important, but also provides connection and communication to further enmesh them in a caring community of learners. We were visiting the school the week in which 5th-graders shared their presentations. Students practiced on us in English before presenting their Cultural Encounter to parents in Icelandic. That they are comfortable using English with adult Americans to describe, narrate, and reflect on who they are is in itself an accomplishment.

An array of individual interests come to life through the Cultural Encounter topics students present. One girl details ballet positions, the construction of toe-shoes, her schedule for practice, classical routines and music that interest her from well-known ballets, and briefly displays her skill, standing on point by the side of her desk. There is a child with a collection of old Norwegian and Icelandic stamps. Another boy, with books of historical maps of the United States and a magnifying glass, explains the regions of the country he and his family visited. A student's storyboards show a series of Donald Duck cartoons he wrote and illustrated. He also includes a brief history of Walt Disney's character. Children present about animals, including domesticated rabbits and cats. An immigrant student from China shares her cultural values and information about clothing, food, celebrations, and religion. A student with a prosthetic leg, involved in skiing at the youth Paralympics, presents information about the technological design of his leg and the Paralympic Games. During his presentation, he tells about his participation at the London games, where he met Oscar Pistorius in 2012. Another student, sharing his interest in the Icelandic justice system, has constructed an elaborate board game, with handmade wooden playing pieces and a deck of informative cards to read when advancing on the board. As part of his collection and research on military vehicles, one child shows us his Lego tank and what it can do. We listen and watch students interact with us and others, and see and hear the intent of the project at work: "promoting mutual respect and understanding between people in a concrete way and through different means of expressions."[5]

Reflecting on the student projects, we see their ability to generate their own ideas, put forward a plan for research, design a format for presenting information, and educate peers and adults about who they are in the world and what holds their ongoing interests. Opening curriculum inquiry to students and supporting the choices they make, including choices about how to investigate and how to report findings, gives voice to students, credits them as meaning-makers, and informs their audiences. Research sources included students' own experiences, interviews with adults and others who engage with them, and online and library searches. Formats for reporting included performance, a board game, poster-boards, computer or iPad screens, handmade books, and speech making. Presentations offered explanations and welcomed questions. "It is expected that through these cultural interactions [students will] develop life-skills that foster the view that ethnic differences make us richer, rather than seeing them as a cause for conflict."[6] The 5th-grade classroom teachers, and Asgeir as well, remark on students' abilities to educate others. In addition to the immediate impact these students' presentations have, the projects are accessible to others as a part of the Library of Reykjavik internet site known as The Flying Carpet—The Cultural Encounter.[7]

### Carousel

Asgeir and his faculty were so pleased with the Cultural Encounter experience with 5th-graders that they wanted to further develop and expand the idea to other grade levels. A 2003 trip to the United States that included a visit to the New Country School in Henderson, Minnesota, allowed them to see project-based learning in action.[8] Their experience provided inspiration. Asgeir and the teachers returned home ready to offer a self-directed learning project to 8th-, 9th-, and 10th-grade students. Hateigsskoli's project is called Carousel, and it is an expanded version of the Cultural Encounter. Asgeir opened a two-hour time block on Wednesdays, giving students time and space for weekly research and planning. Students pick a topic of interest and prepare a project and presentation. A more challenging aspect of the Carousel is that students are expected to connect their topic to all possible curricular areas. Because it is a self-directed learning project, adolescents must find ways in which their interests connect with language arts, science, math, and history. Examples of student topics that we saw were circus performance, Gretta's Icelandic saga, makeup, baking, fashion design, skateboarding, the country and culture of Australia, *Star Wars*, taekwondo, and Malala Yousafzai. Hateigsskoli's take on project-based learning is unique in that high school students are encouraged to include their parents or siblings as contributors to the project. Students with family contributions to the research serve as editors when compiling and reporting findings. In 2013, Hateigsskoli received an Award of Excellence from the Reykjavik Educational Ministry for the project.

### Filmmaking and the Hilmar Awards

Being receptive to ideas means welcoming and responding to students' suggestions for curriculum at Hateigsskoli. A 10th-grade student approached Asgeir with this question: If there could be an Oscar Awards competition and ceremony for film achievement, why not a Hilmar Awards for a competition at the school? It is a testament to the school that adults listen to student ideas for possible inquiry, and that the school's daily schedule and calendar can be flexible enough to accommodate new opportunities. Daniel's question, eight years ago, led to an ongoing film project for 8th- to 10th-graders at Hateigsskoli, which is now a competition for 10th-grade filmmakers in six Reykjavik high schools. A film professor from the University of Iceland, as well as Daniel himself, is involved in judging the competition.

Asgeir values the filmmaking project because "Students and teachers use it to break out of closely defined subject areas." For six weeks, the two-hour time block created for Carousel is reserved for students' creative projects. Tenth-graders organize their own working groups or elect to work alone. If they choose filmmaking, for example, they create a plan. "This is what we will do," Asgeir says, describing the planning steps students consider. "These are the students involved; this is the way we will do it; this is the teacher we have selected to work with us; and this is how we will put forward the results." Students create short films, including animations, about topics of their choice such as veterinarian study; a dog show; the Icelandic Symphony; ice-cream shops; herb curing; anti-bullying; an ABCs film for children; and Batman and Spiderman episodes. In addition to directing and shooting the films, students write scripts, prepare storyboards, and plan for the setting, props, and costumes. "Students do more than we expect," Asgeir tells us.

While experiences such as the Cultural Encounter and Carousel provide opportunities for children to explore their interests, there are other special days in the year that serve to value everyone's strengths, provide mentorship for younger students, and establish a sense of safety and community across all grade levels. One such event is the Multiple Intelligence Days, which take place over two days every other year. Teachers develop a series of 32 seven-minute projects that students work through in heterogeneous teams. Each team is comprised of one student from each grade level. In this arrangement, the 10th-graders are responsible for the 1st- and 2nd-graders, 9th-graders for the 3rd-graders, and the 8th-graders for the 4th-graders. Asgeir explains: "This day of activity establishes respect between age groups, and helps them feel good together."

Looking through pictures of the event on the school website, we see examples of the variety of activities: creating flower canvases for the school that mimic the work of a famous Icelandic painter; spelling games; chess; a reading corner; physical challenges; yoga and practices of mindfulness; coloring Mandala images while soothing music plays; sustainability activities; Cat's Cradle (an old Icelandic game); PhET interactive physics simulations on iPads; and team building are among the activities. The combining of all grade levels is a purposeful choice. By doing so, younger children feel mentored and cared for by "the big kids," which can lead to a trusting and safe environment for them. Older children experience the positive impact they can have on the school environment.

On the school's website, Asgeir points out a picture of a 10th-grader holding a 1st-grader's hand and leading him to their first activity. These interactions, in Asgeir's view, benefit both the older and younger students. "Here was a problem 10th-grade child, but he was being very responsible," he tells us. Later he discussed the same problem student engaging the 1st-grade child in a conversation on sustainability. He was explaining about the chemicals found in many products we use every day. It was obvious to Asgeir that this particular "problem student" was able to see himself as an important and influential member of the school community.

## Roots and Wings

"Stay in school" is a ubiquitous slogan in the United States. It is a message to American youth seen in television commercials, billboards, internet ads, and magazines. It is a slogan meant to inform children of the importance of school and to motivate them to continue. But a slogan to which many would respond: "For what?" Disenchanted, unengaged, and feeling unsuccessful, many students leave, and the door to learning closes. We believe that what we learned at Hateigsskoli—namely, that they have found ways to embrace students' individuality, voices, and gifts so that they can reach their potential, regardless of where it lies—has the capability of keeping that door open for more American children. Students are drawn to school because they are encouraged to be individuals who discover, create, reflect on, and engage in life. They are provided with opportunities to explore themselves and share what they learn with each other. They are provided with a broad and engaging curriculum in which all can find some area of success. And they are immersed in a school that very purposefully creates an environment modeling its value of community and belonging.

Asgeir Beinteinsson recognizes the need for individuals who have a high regard for community to be educated to value and to work using creativity as a critical thinking tool. "We are educating for more than academics," he tells us. "We are educating for lives and democracy." Martha C. Nussbaum (2010), who writes about the importance of liberal arts in K–12 education, shines a light on Asgeir's beliefs, values, and practices. Nussbaum is a philosopher and professor of law and ethics at the University of Chicago. She writes: "Each student must be treated as an individual whose powers of mind are unfolding and who is expected to make an active and creative contribution…" (p. 55). At Hateigsskoli, we saw the value of the individual through creative expression, through sharing of cultures and selves, and through the reflection and community achieved in collaboration. The Cultural Encounter, Carousel, drama productions, and Friday morning sing-alongs depend on confident individuals willing to engage with others while sharing knowledge and abilities. "By emphasizing each person's active voice," Nussbaum writes, "we also promote a culture of accountability. When people see their ideas as their own responsibility, they are more likely, too, to see their deeds as their own responsibility" (p. 54).

Joel Spring (2010), a professor at Queens College in New York City, writes: "Today, a major goal of education [in the United States] is to increase economic growth and prepare students for jobs in the global economy" (p. 7). From the Sputnik-inspired space race of the 1960s, to today's emphasis on science, math, and technology, American education places a premium on traditional academic courses. It is an admirable and important goal. However, Nussbaum (2010) questions this goal and cautions that American education needs the humanities to protect its democracy. She prefers a curriculum that champions the arts, discovery, and creativity, and that addresses the whole individual—connecting students to the humanities to best serve democracy (Nussbaum, 2010). In light of the recent rise in strong nationalist and populist themes in both European and American politics, giving rise to such broad-brush generalizations as xenophobic and isolationist attitudes, Hateigsskoli's call for something other than highly focused academic courses seems admirable and important.

Icelanders, who formed the world's first parliament, actively participate in their contemporary democracy. The public outcry for reform after the 2008 economic crisis is known as the Pots and Pans Rebellion, because citizens filled the streets in front of government buildings, beating pots and pans with spoons, voicing demands for change. The April 2016 release of the Panama Papers brought people with pots, pans, and demands to the streets once more. With democracy a cultural value, as well as a theme across the curriculum, it is not surprising to find a public educated and willing to challenge government by openly voicing alternatives to the status quo.

At Hateigsskoli, Asgeir, the teachers, and the students are cognizant of democracy and connect it to curriculum vigorously, something American education seems to do halfheartedly. We find Hateigsskoli to be in support of Nussbaum's (2010) belief that education should be for the whole individual and that it must reconnect students to the humanities to best serve democracy. Though the contemporary aim of American public education is to position students and the nation for global economic success, Nussbaum warns that "educators for economic growth will do more than ignore the arts. They will fear them" (p. 23).

Nussbaum links creativity to democracy, concepts entwined as themes to be included in all Icelandic curricula at all grade levels. She cites India's famed early 20th-century educator, writing: "Tagore said, aggressive nationalism needs to blunt the moral conscience, so it needs people who do not recognize the individual, who speak group-speak, who behave and see the world like docile bureaucrats. Art is a great enemy of that obtuseness, and artists (unless thoroughly browbeaten and corrupted) are not the reliable servants of any ideology…" (pp. 23–24). With an aim of education for economic growth, educators "will campaign against the humanities and arts as ingredients for basic education" (p. 24). The shortchanging of the arts is already evident in American education.

Hateigsskoli seems to prove that arts and the core curriculum need not be viewed as an X vs. Y dichotomy. Students at Hateigsskoli spend as much time in academic classes as they do in classes that many Americans would consider non-academic. They value and emphasize creativity and self-expression, as well as learning disciplinary knowledge. And while their students perform less well than American students in reading, it is important to note that they perform better than American students in math, according to the latest Program for International Student Assessment (PISA) test scores, published in 2015.[9] While it cannot be claimed that the inclusion of the arts and humanities causes higher math scores, it does provide a strong counterexample for those who would argue that the arts and humanities must be pared to allow more time to improve math performance.

Perhaps even more important than rankings and test scores should be the consideration of our children's quality of life while in school. Perhaps more effort should be placed on providing a curriculum that would impact a wider variety of students with various strengths, interests, backgrounds, and needs; a curriculum developed for a diverse population in which all types of individuals could find some place of passion for themselves; a curriculum compelling enough to provide students with the motivation to stay in school, keeping the doors to learning open.

Educators often laud successful models but go on to focus on why such models would not be successful in a different environment. For example, educators marvel at the achievement in Finnish education but balk when considering the practices that lead to those results. Some of these practices include selecting only the top 10% of applicants to teacher education programs, abandoning homework and testing in elementary and secondary schools, and seeking multiple avenues toward creativity in students' curricula (Sahlberg, 2015). Finnish ideas are discounted by those who say, in part, that Finland is small and homogeneous—so different from the United States—that their models could not be useful to inform American practices. Some may say the same about what we saw and learned in Iceland because Icelandic education serves a small, homogeneous population.

Size and homogeneous environment are not sufficient reasons to discount promising practices. We question why more curricular offerings, more opportunity for creativity, expression, reflection, and interaction would be less applicable to a heterogeneous population. Why exploration of self and others would prove less advantageous within a diverse community. Why educating creative, self-directed critical thinkers would not lead to fulfilling personal lives for individuals able to foster democracy and private enterprise. Perhaps for American education, a focus on democracy (Dewey, 1916) and core content areas could provide the roots that our students need.

And perhaps a focus on further developing and integrating these within a more intensive exploration of the arts, humanities, self, and community could provide the wings.

## Notes

1. See http://www.hateigsskoli.is/
2. See http://www.hateigsskoli.is/
3. See http://www.hateigsskoli.is/
4. See http://borgarbokasafn.is/en/content/flying-carpet-intercultural-gatherings
5. See http://borgarbokasafn.is/en/content/flying-carpet-intercultural-gatherings
6. See http://borgarbokasafn.is/en/content/flying-carpet-intercultural-gatherings
7. See http://borgarbokasafn.is/en/content/flying-carpet-intercultural-gatherings
8. See http://www.newcountryschool.com/about-mnc/ mncs-design-elements/
9. See https://nces.ed.gov/surveys/pisa/pisa2015/pisa2015highlights_5.asp

## References

Agnarsdottir, Frida. (2013, May 22). Interview.

Agnarsdottir, Frida. (2013, May 23). Interview.

Agnarsdottir, Frida. (2016, April 27). Interview.

Beinteinsson, Asgeir. (2009, May 24). Interview.

Beinteinsson, Asgeir. (2010, May 27). Interview.

Beinteinsson, Asgeir. (2013, May 21). Interview.

Beinteinsson, Asgeir. (2013, May 22). Interview.

Beinteinsson, Asgeir. (2013, May 23). Interview.

Beinteinsson, Asgeir. (2016, April 25). Interview.

Beinteinsson, Asgeir. (2016, April 26). Interview.

Beinteinsson, Asgeir. (2016, April 27). Interview.

Beinteinsson, Asgeir. (2016, April 29). Interview.

Byram, M. (1997). *Teaching and assessing intercultural communicative competence*. Bristol, PA: Multilingual Matters Ltd.

Dewey, J. (1916). *Democracy and education*. New York: Macmillan.

Einarsdottir, Gudny. (2010, May 27). Interview.

Einarsdottir, Gudny. (2013, May 22). Interview.

Einarsdottir, Gudny. (2013, May 23). Interview.

Einarsdottir, Gudny. (2016, April 27). Interview.

Einarsdottir, Gudny. (2016, April 29). Interview.

Gnarr, J. (2014). *Gnarr! How I became the mayor of a large city in Iceland and changed the world*. Brooklyn, NY: Melville House.

Gudjonsdottir, Hulda. (2010, May 27). Interview.

Gudjonsdottir, Hulda. (2013, May 22). Interview.

Gudjonsdottir, Hulda. (2013, May 23). Interview.

Gudjonsdottir, Hulda. (2016, April 26). Interview.

Gudjonsdottir, Hulda. (2016, April 27). Interview.

Gudjonsdottir, Hulda. (2016, April 29). Interview.

Nussbaum, M.C. (2010). *Not for profit: Why democracy needs the humanities*. Princeton, NJ: Princeton University Press.

Sahlberg, P. (2014). *Finnish lessons 2.0: What can the world learn from educational change in Finland?* (2nd ed.). New York: Teachers College Press.

Smart-Morstad, K.J., & Triggs, S.B. (2007). Dismissed potential: Why kids "hate" school. In S.P. Jones, C.J. Pearman, & E.C. Sheffield (Eds.), *Why kids hate school* (pp. 97–105). Dubuque, IA: Kendall/Hunt.

Spring, J. (2010). *American education: Sociocultural, political, and historical studies in education* (15th ed.). New York: Routledge.

# CHAPTER EIGHT

# A MANUAL ON HOW TO MAKE CHILDREN HATE SCHOOL

## The Case of Test-Driven Chinese Education

LIANG ZHAO

THE PAST DECADE HAS witnessed an increase in standards and testing in the United States. Government officials want to hold schools accountable and see results, and teachers and school administrators feel pressure to improve student learning, which is now usually measured by student scores on standardized tests. Many teachers and school administrators have heard that Chinese students test well in international student achievement comparisons, and they may wonder if they can learn some tricks from Chinese educators so that their own students will test well, too. American educators don't know much about why Chinese students test well, and they may not realize how damaging China's testing system is to student development, or how it makes children hate school.

If you want children to hate school, implement the test-driven practices used in China. School will become boring and tiring, and children won't go to school because it is a fun place to be. They will go because they have to. But if you want children to love school, don't adopt the high-stakes testing model. This model takes away all the fun parts of learning: exploration, discovery, self-expression, and ownership of learning.

In this chapter I will explore the astonishing school practices used in China, but first I will explain why China has such a model of education. Further, I will explain the sociological and economic reasons for the testing model.

## What Is Test-Driven Education, and Why Does China Use It?

Test-driven education refers to a model of schooling in which everything revolves around testing. High test scores are the ultimate goal of teaching and learning, and testing drives educational decisions. In this model, students study hard to get high test scores, teachers work hard so that their students can test well, and school administrators and government officials use test scores to prove they have done their job.

China has a long history of selecting public servants through testing. The modern-day testing system permeates every aspect of economic life. It is through testing that students get into schools, graduate from schools, enroll in professional training programs, and enter various professions. The high-stakes testing model, in this sense, is for ensuring equal opportunity—one can compete for wealth and social status if one is able to learn and is willing to work hard, no matter which social class one is born into. In this sense, the high-stakes testing model works in China just as it works in the United States. The difference is that, in China, many more people compete for many fewer resources, which results in fiercer competition for educational opportunities.

### Competition for Opportunities

Although China and the United States occupy similar land areas, the population density of China is four times that of the United States. But the gross domestic production (GDP) per capita of China is only one-seventh that of the United States. This means that more people are competing for limited wealth. For most people, the only way to move up socially is through education. "[T]he [educational] system determines people's livelihood. Because it is the only path to social mobility, people follow it eagerly" (Zhao, 2014, p. 122). The Chinese educational system is a high-stakes testing model, which means students must test well to be enrolled in a better school at every level of schooling.

Graduating from college no longer guarantees a job. A recent report indicated that, in China, 20% of new college graduates were unable to secure a full-time job within six months (*Guangming Daily*, 2015). One has to graduate from a *good* college to increase his or her chances for employment. Of course, one first has to be *admitted* to a good college. One's college placement is determined almost solely by a single factor: performance on the College Entrance Exam (CEE), a test that is offered only once a year, in June. A student's performance on the CEE correlates closely with the quality of the high school from which that student graduates. High schools are tiered, and a student has to score well to get into a high-tier school. Middle schools and elementary schools are tiered, too. Therefore, competition for better schools begins before the 1st grade. Simply put, students must compete against their peers to get into a good elementary school; then they compete to get into a good middle school, then a good high school, and, finally, a good college. In order to make a better living in their adulthood, students compete against each other all through their educational careers to get the highest test scores possible at every level of schooling. This is the fundamental reason why Chinese students work so hard and test so well. The function of schooling is getting students into better schools at the next level of schooling by way of test preparation. So, testing drives the school system.

American educators need to understand that school quality varies considerably, even within the same school district, because China has practiced "tracking" for a few decades. Tracking in the United States takes place within a school, and the Chinese do that, too. But, more important, they funnel students into different schools based on prior educational achievement. They have regular schools and "priority" schools (*zhongdian xuexiao*). Priority schools admit the most talented students, have more funding, and attract the highest-quality teachers; thus, both the best human resources and physical resources are concentrated in priority schools. This method of tracking is most efficient in training the most talented students to become workers in the industries that are key to the nation's ability to build its capacity. It is undemocratic in Americans' eyes, but China is working on efficiency, not equality.

### The Social Efficiency Orientation

The above analysis explains what motivates students to work hard and what motivates their parents to push them to learn more and test better. From the government's point of view, education is a means to improve social efficiency (Kliebard, 2004). Simply put, this philosophy holds that schools should teach only what students will use in their future occupations. In other words, education should serve the economy, and it should teach the knowledge and skills demanded by industry. This is in sharp contrast to the philosophy of developmentalism, which emphasizes the cognitive, social-emotional, physical, and moral development of the child. Guided by the social efficiency philosophy, schools provide knowledge and skills based on their utility in building the nation's capacity to create wealth and compete in the global economy, and such knowledge and skills are vigorously tested. Students become "human capital," an instrument for economic growth. In this model, schools are not for children, but for the economy. For this reason, children don't find school enjoyable. School is not something to be enjoyed; it is where you get the job done. It is a necessary evil.

## School Practices That Make Children Hate School

The school practices I am about to describe are in place because of the test-driven model of education. These practices are the result of the competition for opportunities and the social efficiency orientation, discussed above, and they result from the current developmental stage of the nation and its population density. I argue that these practices cause children to dislike school.

### Long School Days

The school day for Chinese students is much longer than that of their American counterparts. It is difficult for American educators to imagine that, in China, a principal—and even a homeroom teacher—can decide on adding extra periods in the morning before school starts or in the evening after school ends. There is no teacher's union, and there is no contract to negotiate. In most cases, elementary school students stay in school for about 7 hours a day, middle school students for about 10 hours, and high school students for about 12 hours (Butrymowicz, 2011).

Elementary school typically starts at 8 A.M. and ends at 5 P.M., with a two-hour lunch break from noon to 2 P.M. Middle school students start at 7 A.M. and end at 5 P.M., with the same kind of lunch break. But they typically go back to school from 7 to 9 P.M. for extra sessions. High school students have the same schedule as do middle school students, but their extra sessions typically last until 11 P.M.

The extra sessions before and after the formal school day are voluntary, at least theoretically. Parents must pay an extra fee for them, and almost all students attend them. During these sessions, teachers typically lecture on academic content, just as in any other period of the day, and that's why students believe they have to attend them. High schools usually have seven or eight official periods a day, but most schools have a study hall before the first period, one after the last period, and three or four periods in the evening after dinner. My nephew's high school, for example, starts at 7 A.M. and does not end until 9 P.M. He does not come home for lunch or dinner (which can be purchased in school) during the two breaks built into the schedule. He stays in school for 14 hours a day.

Chinese children stay in school longer than their parents stay at work. A survey by the Chinese Youth and Children Research Center revealed that, on average, China's children spend 8.6 hours a day at school, with some spending 12 hours a day in the classroom (*China Daily*, 2007). As a result, children do not have time to do other things, such as playing outside with friends. With the school schedule they endure, students either have no time to play, have no one to play with, or are too tired to play. More than half of those surveyed said a good night's sleep was what they wanted the most.

One may wonder why the Chinese keep their children in school for so long each day. Chinese students spend almost every minute available to boost their test scores. Studying in the classroom, with or without teachers, is certainly more effective and efficient than studying at home. Time spent studying ties in with our previous discussion. Fundamentally, students must have good test scores to get into a better school at a higher level of schooling, and eventually into a good college. Parents want their children to go to good colleges and get well-paying jobs. Teachers want their students to test well so that their own evaluations and pay will not be compromised. Principals and government officials want their schools to test well so that they can claim accomplishments. Educators have tried every way possible to boost student test scores, and lengthening the school day has been shown to work.

### Frequent Tests

Most middle schools and high schools in China have weekly tests and monthly tests—and, needless to say, midterm and final exams. These tests are school-wide or district-wide. Students also take state-wide tests, especially before entering the next level of schooling. Test results are widely reported, and everyone is judged by results from these tests—teachers, administrators, and government officials. Testing is an integral part of school life. As a popular saying goes, "Testing, testing, and testing—testing is a teacher's secret weapon. Score, score, and score—score is a student's life line." American testing is usually a state mandate, but in China, schools and districts are the ones pushing testing—and, even more often, teachers are the ones wanting to test students. Teachers and principals believe that testing will often reveal where lapses or weaknesses are and will eventually raise student test scores. But frequent testing also makes learning uninteresting, and it makes children dislike school.

## Rote Memorization for Tests

For teachers in the classroom, it is a practical question as to what to teach and how to teach it. Because of the urgency of testing, teachers often teach only what will be tested—that is, they teach to the test. In the English classroom, for example, listening to and speaking English get little attention—this because these skills are not tested, or they constitute only a tiny portion of a test. The bulk of the final tests examine students on what they know about grammar and how well they can read and comprehend English. These, then, are the things teachers emphasize in their teaching. The result of this way of teaching English is that students test well, but they are unable to speak the language or understand someone who speaks the language.

A related issue is how to teach something. Teachers and students have discovered that rote memorization is most effective in raising test scores. Therefore, students spend much time memorizing new words, grammar rules, and even the entirety of texts. Being able to speak a foreign language is fun, but memorizing words, rules, and texts is not fun. However, neither teachers nor students want to "waste" time on something that will not be tested. The emphasis on rote memorization contributes to children's dislike of school.

The following account is offered by Zixuan Zhang, a 9th-grade student in China. This account helps explain the role that memorization plays in education:

> The most important exam in the 8th grade was the Geography-Biology Combined Test, because its score would become a component of the High School Entrance Exam, which would determine if we were able to enroll in a high school. We began to memorize, from the 2nd semester of 8th grade, geography and biology facts. Every morning we arrived at school at 6:30, and read and memorized geography and biology for 30 minutes. And before the Combined Test, another period in the afternoon was designated for reading and memorizing geography and biology.

You may have noticed that Zhang's school day started at 6:30 A.M. In that particular school, the first period officially started at 8:10, but the school decided to add a study hall starting at 7:10. In addition, Zhang's homeroom teacher decided to add another session starting at 6:30, so that students could recite geography and biology facts for the combined exam. Students in that middle school were dismissed at 6:20 P.M. It was a rural school, and evening sessions were impossible. Both principals and homeroom teachers have the authority to lengthen the school day.

### Despising Low-Performing Students

Test scores are very important to everyone involved in education in China— students, teachers, administrators, government officials, and parents. And students with high test scores are considered good students, which makes parents and everyone else proud. Everyone likes these students. But it is also true that low-performing students are despised by just about everyone, making their lives miserable. When the average score of the class is what everyone considers most important, low-performing students are a burden. Dropping out of school is sometimes the natural escape for these students.

I will describe a strange phenomenon (to the eyes of most Americans) that can demonstrate how teachers and schools cherish high performers and, to some extent, how they view low performers. Each year, many students repeat their senior year because their test scores are not high enough to get them into a good college. However, they look forward to the advantages a second year will give them—not just because they think they will score better on the College Entrance Exam (more of an achievement test than an aptitude test), but because they know they will be competing for spots in better schools with students who are now a full year younger than they are. Many high schools will do anything to enroll these second-chance students who, educators believe, will test well the next year and therefore enhance the reputation of their school. These "success stories" are taken to be signs of the school's "accomplishment," and this brings more funding and more high performers from feeder schools, thus perpetuating the success story the school wants to tell and believe.

Most schools rank their students from top to bottom. Schools send this ranking report—complete with everyone's name and rank in a given grade—to every student's home. In my nephew's high school, students take home a report at midterm and at the end of the year. On that report, the following things are listed: every student's test score in every subject, the total score for every student, and their ranking in their grade. Although this is against government policy, it is a widely used practice. Some homeroom teachers post the ranking on the wall in the homeroom to "motivate" the low performers to work harder and move up their ranking. The downside is obvious: the low performers don't like school for this reason.

Some teachers seat students by test score. Often, high performers get to sit at the front of the room, and teachers tell low performers to sit at the back. Teachers say they want to "reward" high performers with "better" seats, but the unspoken message is clear: teachers will focus on the high performers, who are promising and will bring fame and glory to the teachers and the school, instead of "wasting time" on the low performers.

It is common for teachers to scold, blame, or ridicule students for not being able to grasp academic content in a subject area. Although it is a less common practice, some teachers hit students for the same reason. I personally encountered such a case when I was doing fieldwork in a rural elementary school in the northwest in 2013. I was given an office in the building, and across the hallway from the office was a 3rd-grade classroom. One day I noticed a problem in that classroom. I heard a math teacher hitting her student, and so I investigated. I found out later that the teacher had called the student to the front of the room to work a math problem on the chalkboard. The student was not able to solve the problem, so the teacher hit him. I heard the student cry and beg the teacher to stop.

You may wonder how a teacher could justify hitting a student. In China, if a student has failed to learn something the teacher has tried to teach him or her, teachers generally consider it the student's fault. But what is no doubt more important in this particular school district is that teacher evaluation, and teaching assignments, are tied to student test scores. "Incompetent" teachers—as measured, of course, by student test scores—are likely to be assigned to remote, low-performing schools with undesirable working conditions. In other words, low-performing students hurt their teachers' standing.

In the United States over the last few years, more and more states have adopted the policy of linking teacher evaluation to student test performance. In Louisiana, for example, teacher evaluation is based on two factors, each counting for 50% of the teacher's evaluation: student test score and principal observation (Beabout & Chiasson, 2017). Many argue that teacher evaluation ought to be tied to merit pay. In China, student test scores are connected to teacher evaluation, promotion, and winning awards. It is widely believed that "good" teachers are those whose students score high on tests, and these "good" teachers are promoted to a higher rank and receive more pay. "Good" teachers win all kinds of awards, which elevates their status. This gives them the opportunity to transfer to better schools and makes them highly sought-after by parents and principals. This, in turn, drives up their fees for after-school tutoring.

Every teacher wants to be seen as being a "good" teacher, especially new teachers who are eager to establish themselves. Teachers like high-performing students because they boost the average test score of the class, and teachers recognize how low-performing students "drag" the class average lower. This situation gets heightened when teachers are compared to one another—and when teachers, administrators, and everyone else studies the test scores to see whose class average is higher and which teacher has the most top students in the grade. I remember my own experience when I first began teaching in China in my early twenties. I felt that I needed to prove to others that I was a good teacher, at least as good as other teachers. I realized that if I could raise the scores of low-performing students in my classes, my class average would rise. I implemented a strategy to help the low performers improve by focusing on them and calling on them more often to answer questions or to perform certain tasks—this, to get them ready for the test. Often these students did not know the answer or could not perform the task, and I realized that my pressuring these students had become depressing for everyone. I had trapped myself into thinking that the low-performing students were in the way of my achieving excellence in teaching. Now I know better. We cannot determine excellence in teaching by examining class averages. Excellence has much more to do with working hard with individual students, with setting targets for each student and helping each one to reach that target. Educating has to mean much more than getting students ready for tests.

## Conclusion

The United States is on the way to more and more testing. When teachers and administrators are under heightened pressure to raise student test scores, they are prone to seek what appear to be easy ways out. We saw an example of this in Atlanta, Georgia, where the former superintendent of the Atlanta Public Schools and many school administrators "improved" student test scores through cheating (Zhao, 2014). More and more teachers have discovered that teaching to the test is, in the short run, effective in boosting student test scores. Teachers may institute other practices that raise test scores but harm students and their learning. Teachers may start doing something similar to what the Chinese do without knowing the consequences. I argue that educators ought not to focus on test scores, but instead focus on *learning*. When students have truly learned knowledge and skills, they will not score poorly on tests.

The pursuit of high test scores, in the Chinese way, results in the loss of individuality and creativity on the part of the students and makes them hate school. The price of high test scores is too high. Worthier goals are true student learning, student growth and development, and student self-actualization. American educators should avoid practices that alienate students, such as overemphasis on class ranking, rote memorization, frequent tests, lengthening of the school day, and despising low-performing students.

American educators should continue doing the great things they often do, such as focusing on student development, creativity, and self-expression, and they should avoid practices that are test-driven. The United States has many great educators. One of them, Rafe Esquith, a 5th-grade teacher in Los Angeles, has gained a great deal of attention. He has done some marvelous things with students, such as reading full-length, challenging books, learning music, doing year-long art projects, having one period of P.E. every day, traveling to historical sites, and producing a different Shakespeare play each year (Esquith, 2007). This is a better model to emulate.

American educators have been known for doing many things right, which is one of the reasons that so many Chinese students come to the United States to study at the K–12 level. American education at this level is viewed as freeing the child, promoting individuality, and encouraging self-expression. American education has been dedicated to developing the whole child—not only intellectually, but also socially, emotionally, morally, and spiritually. We should keep doing what we have been doing well and avoid going any further in the direction of more standards and testing. I hope the present chapter on test-driven education in China reminds readers of the damage that can be done using such an approach.

I also need to inform readers that China's education is becoming more and more diversified, and some schools (though not many) have begun to challenge the testing model. One alternative model is the classical school (Zhao, 2015), which teaches the Chinese classics, martial arts, calligraphy, traditional painting, and traditional musical instruments. Like much of American education, this model emphasizes developing the whole child, her capacity to use her senses, and her acquisition of noble ideals. In the example of this classical school, perhaps American educators can learn good things from China. But as I look at the high international test scores coming from China, I earnestly hope that Americans won't choose to follow the example of China's test-driven model of schooling.

## References

Beabout, B., & Chiasson, J. (2017, March). *Lessons from teacher evalua-tion reform in Louisiana.* Paper presented at the Critical Questions in Education Conference, New Orleans, LA.

Butrymowicz, S. (2011). A day in the life of Chinese students. *The Henchinger Report.* Available at http://hechingerreport.org/a-day-in-the-life-of-chinese-students/.

*China Daily.* (2007, May 13). China's children too busy for playtime. Available at http://www.chinadaily.com.cn/china/2007-05/13/content_871182.htm

Esquith, R. (2007). *Teach like your hair's on fire: The methods and madness inside Room 56.* New York: Viking.

*Guangming Daily.* (2015, July 17). 自主创业持续上升" 重心下沉" 趋势初显 [More college graduates are self-employed, and more are in smaller towns]. Available at http://tech.gmw.cn/2015-07/17/content_16330179.htm

Kliebard, H.M. (2004). *The struggle for the American curriculum: 1893–1958* (3rd ed.). New York: RoutledgeFalmer.

Zhao, L. (2015, February). *Classical education in contemporary China: A case study.* Paper presented at the Critical Questions in Education Conference, San Diego, CA.

Zhao, Y. (2014). *Who's afraid of the big bad dragon? Why China has the best (and worst) education system in the world.* San Francisco, CA: Jossey-Bass.

# CHAPTER NINE

# IGNITING PASSION AMONG STUDENTS (AND TEACHERS) FOR CIVIC ENGAGEMENT

## The Role of Communities of Practice

GARY A. HOMANA

> *Public education does not serve a public. It creates a public. And in creating the right kind of public, the schools contribute to strengthening the spiritual basis of the American creed.... The question is not "Does or doesn't public school create a public?" The question is, "What kind of public does it create?"*
>
> —Neil Postman (1996)

SCHOOLS PLAY A CRITICAL role in the education of our young people. While the development of academic abilities has been a primary focus of schools, they also assist students in understanding society and prepare them for civic engagement. Despite growing interest in promoting opportunities for students to develop into politically aware and civically responsible citizens, educating for civic engagement in the United States has been increasingly threatened by "high-stakes" strategies aimed at raising academic achievement, particularly in the lower grades and in schools that serve historically disadvantaged populations. These reforms, which hold schools accountable for achievement in a select set of subjects, have encouraged what has been referred to as a "narrowing of the curriculum." Curriculum material not tested is excluded by teachers and schools in order to maximize test scores on the material that is tested. At issue is the extent of change in curriculum and instructional time for both tested and non-tested subject areas, with the emphasis placed on tested subjects, such as reading and math, at the expense of other subjects, including civic education, social studies, and history.

Young people are naturally inquisitive and passionate, and want to engage in meaningful learning activities that improve their lives and communities. Students are yearning to engage in active learning, participate in open discussions about social and political issues, experience for themselves having a voice in the school as a whole, and extend their learning beyond the school to address real community issues. When learning environments focus heavily on high-stakes standardized tests, however, students have limited opportunities to think and write critically or become actively involved in civic-related issues. This high-stakes testing environment also limits the creativity, imagination, and possibilities for learning that can occur when students interact and learn from one another.

Research suggests the value of the association between the social structures in schools and civic capacities (e.g., Torney-Purta, Homana, & Barber, 2006). As structures where learning is embedded in social experiences, schools can be powerful places in which classroom activities simultaneously create normative expectations and forms of interactions supportive of students' academic and civic development. Although the socially embedded nature of schooling can constrain learning, it can also create opportunities where students and adults come together to understand a range of views and opinions. Additionally, it can cultivate attitudes and behaviors that contribute to the common good and the renewal of democratic societies. As such, schools are uniquely poised to facilitate students' understanding of how to engage in a range of political and nonpolitical activities that promote democratic ends. From this perspective, the relationship between the social structures of schools and the development of student capacities for civic engagement can be seen as a link between educational practices and a healthy democratic society.

Emerging efforts to understand learning have led to an interest in the mediating role of culture and social context in the academic and cognitive growth of children. This perspective, sometimes referred to as the socio-cultural perspective (Vygotsky, 1986), has the potential to bridge concerns about enhancing learning in both core subject areas and civic development. One such approach to understanding the culture and social context is the notion of "communities of practice" (Lave & Wenger, 1991, 2001; Wenger, 1998, 2014). This construct focuses on the social organization of groups, including the interactions of students and adults that affect the learning of young people.

## Communities of Practice

Communities of practice can be seen as social places or structures where-in students practice what it means to be thoughtful and engaged members of society. From this perspective, the power of a particular community of practice rests with the nature of the learning opportunities it creates for students. Although not all communities provide positive environments for civic engagement, for the work presented in this chapter, communities of practice, by definition, represent a positive, inclusive, safe, and healthy learning environment for students.

In communities of practice for civic engagement, students come together to discuss common concerns and interact to sustain mutual agreement on issues. At the same time, they serve to build mutual trust and respect, help students to develop individual identities, and encourage meaningful engagement in the social world. In these communities of practice, students are encouraged to make up their own minds about civic issues and to feel free to express their opinions, even when their opinions differ from those of most other students. Students learn to understand the views of others, cooperate in groups, and act together to solve problems in their schools and neighborhoods. For these reasons, communities of practice offer a way to understand the challenges and possibilities associated with encouraging forms of civic learning that promote positive social and cultural norms for the betterment of the student, the school, and society.

Central to the original conceptualization of communities of practice is the process of *legitimate peripheral participation*. For Lave and Wenger, learning is an integral part of the generative social and cultural practices that create and sustain learning communities over time. Legitimate peripheral participation can be seen as that part of the learning process through which individuals engage in and begin to understand the social and cultural practices of a community—for example, common language, knowledge, and experiences. In this way, individuals identify, share, and develop a context for learning as members of the group (in this case, a classroom or school). Legitimate peripheral participation is a transformational process through which newer members of a community move from being novices to becoming experts of the community. For schools, this suggests that communities of practice are where students develop and practice the civic capacities that transform them from novices to competent citizens—prepared to address their civic responsibilities as adults.

Communities of practice in school can serve to promote positive student civic engagement by re-imagining the possibilities of teaching so that students have the opportunity to actively engage in meaningful and authentic learning. This approach includes the development of a range of civic competencies related not just to the acquisition of knowledge, but also to the development of attitudes, dispositions, and skills for active and meaningful civic participation.

## Refining Communities of Practice

Utilizing a refined conceptualization of Lave and Wenger's notion of communities of practice, this chapter explores the potential of three distinct and positive dimensions of a healthy school community (Homana, 2009) to ignite the passion for civic engagement among our youth. These dimensions include the *discourse community*, the *collaborative community*, and the *participatory community*, which at their core emphasize quality learning experiences intended to foster a positive transition for students from novice to civically motivated and competent individuals.

### The Discourse Community of Practice

This community focuses on students as they do the cognitive work related to engaging in dialogues and discussions with other students and their teachers, initially in the classroom but also extending to other school activities. In the discourse community, students interact to sustain mutual agreement on common civic concerns. Meaningful civic learning can occur within the context of participation in a school's discourse communities. As such, this community of practice can serve as a bridge for civic engagement because it can help facilitate common understandings and opportunities for dialogue leading to support for civic responsibility.

Through group membership and participation, the discourse community of practice supports the development of meaningful civic knowledge relevant to action. Torney-Purta and Richardson (2003) articulate three features necessary for meaningful civic learning: (1) students' past understandings are made authentic by connections to current issues and concerns; (2) students' construction of their own civic knowledge contributes to higher levels of civic understanding; and (3) discussion and dialogue promote an open exchange of ideas where students listen and build on others' opinions.

At the same time, instructional practice on student civic outcomes deserves attention. Even though there is a call for deeper student engagement with civic topics where teachers utilize more constructivist techniques, it appears that most teachers predominantly utilize traditional rather than more interactive and experiential methods. Homana and Passe (2013) found that while elementary, middle, and high school social studies teachers believe developing the civic capacities of students is a crucial goal, most still utilize the lecture as the primary form of instruction. Other evidence has revealed lower-level student thinking, a narrow knowledge base, and few substantive opportunities to discuss how a robust democracy is connected to addressing civic problems (Kahne, Rodriquez, Smith, & Thiede, 2000). At the same time, barriers often exist that limit the opportunities for discussing controversial issues in schools. Teachers, for example, may fear a backlash from the community if the discussion is too controversial, they feel ill-prepared to use this type of pedagogy, or they do not have the necessary in-school support to conduct the work (Hess & Avery, 2008).

All students require meaningful opportunities to develop their capacity for civic engagement and their sense of civic identity. According to Wenger (1998), meaningful learning is central to human identity. In the discourse community, the meaning constructed by the individual is shaped by and helps to shape the community in which students come together as a group to understand, interact, and make sense out of what they are learning and how it applies to their lives and the world around them.

## The Collaborative Community of Practice

This dimension of community of practice for civic engagement emphasizes a safe and cooperative school environment based on trust, collaboration, and respect among its members. Underlying these demands are supportive relationships and positive perceptions of the school environment. Two areas of interest have implications for the collaborative community's role in educating for civic engagement—student-teacher and student-student relationships, and student perceptions of the school as a caring community.

Teachers viewed by students as caring can positively influence students' academic efforts and pursuit of social responsibility. Students who feel valued and cared for by their teachers also hold beliefs associated with positive developmental outcomes such as the importance of having high expectations, seeking opportunities for autonomous decision-making, and promoting democratic interaction styles (Wentzel, 1997, 1998). Similarly, caring teachers positively influence both students' views about and interest in attending school and their beliefs about their classroom environment (Brown, Powell, & Clark, 2012).

Peers and friends among adolescents also have an important influence on the nature of collaborative communities because of the role these relationships play in the development of responsibility. Wentzel (1994) found that students who receive academic support from peers also appear to have positive attitudes about sharing, helping each other, and keeping promises and commitments—all important traits for civic responsibility. In addition, students' peers and friends can have a strong influence on motivation and the cultivation of shared values to succeed in school (e.g., Wentzel, Barry, & Caldwell, 2004). More recently, a meta-analysis of eight decades' worth of research strongly supports the association of more positive peer relationships and higher academic outcomes with this type of community in school (Roseth, Johnson, & Johnson, 2008).

Classroom teachers who create caring learning environments marked by mutual respect, collaboration, and increased pupil voice can positively influence student awareness of issues related to identity, power, and social control (Gifford, Watt, Clark, & Koster, 2005; Urdan & Schoenfelder, 2006). This may be especially relevant concerning social, ethnic, and cultural identity issues. As such, teaching focused on educating students for civic engagement suggests the importance of classroom learning environments reflecting open discourse and democratic participation.

Mutual trust has consistently appeared as a key characteristic of schools associated with a range of positive student developmental outcomes. In fact, it may be the most significant component in the creation of positive and caring learning environments leading to a range of positive student developmental outcomes such as concern for others, conflict resolution, social competence, motivation, and engagement (e.g., Battistich, Solomon, Watson, & Schaps, 1997; Cappella, Neal, & Sahu, 2012).

When students explore their own values, convictions, and beliefs through authentic learning with others, they may also enhance their attitudes and motivation toward civic engagement. The collaborative community of practice can help provide a strong foundation for developing the necessary civic dispositions of students and help them make positive judgments and commitment to the broader civic community. It may also be a vehicle to help teachers and other members of the school understand the importance of—and increase their commitment to—creating these types of collaborations across the schools. These collaborations can help to build a strong and positive school environment and foster both academic and civic learning outcomes.

### The Participatory Community of Practice

This community emphasizes active involvement in experiences that provide distinct opportunities for students to engage in action and change. In the participatory community, students practice the skills and behaviors that are associated with the discourse and collaborative communities and utilize them in addressing real problems in their schools and neighborhoods. In this community of practice, students work together to examine civic issues around which they engage in decision-making and participate in meaningful change.

Schools serve as important places to help cultivate student civic participation. When students connect what they are learning in the classroom to real problems in their schools or neighborhoods, they are not only more likely to become actively engaged and motivated in learning but also to recognize the importance of their contributions to society. Students who engage in curriculum-connected community service such as service-learning display greater trust, tolerance, and commitment to service, and they tend to believe they can make a difference in their communities (e.g., Kennedy & Mellor, 2006; Ludden, 2011; Torney-Purta, Amadeo, & Richardson, 2007). This type of curriculum-connected service is also a predictor of expected civic participation, valuing school, and high levels of academic motivation (Billig, Root, & Jesse, 2005; Kahne & Sporte, 2008). Additional research has found support for participation in peaceful protests and youth-focused forums (Kahne, Crow, & Lee, 2013).

Issues of power and authority in school can be detrimental to the types of positive experiences associated with the participatory community of practice intended to foster full democratic engagement (Levinson & Brantmeier, 2006). In practical terms, these issues can translate into dilemmas of how students learn to navigate and participate in an environment where teachers' or principals' authority is dominant and where apprentice-like experiences for cultivating youth voice, decision-making, and leadership are limited.

Youth voice is a critical component related to all three dimensions of communities of practice. Yet youth voice and youth participation in school decision-making are largely non-existent. It is important to include students as active participants so that they can express opinions that are respected and listened to and make decisions regarding school and neighborhood-related concerns. In this way, they experience the consequences of those decisions and develop civic leadership skills that help improve their schools as learning environments. Active student participation in schools can lead to positive student outcomes. These opportunities can occur both within the classroom and school-wide.

In conclusion, the refined notions of communities of practice—the *discourse community*, the *collaborative community*, and the *participatory community*—can enhance the school's role in the development of student civic engagement. The framework is offered as a way to incorporate communities of practice into educational instructional practices to re-engage students in their learning and re-awaken their love of school. By doing so, communities of practice can help promote not only academic and civic development but positive social and cultural norms for the betterment of the students, the school, and society.

## Communities of Practice in the Classroom and School: Making Learning Come Alive

Creating communities of practice that inspire students to explore and discover (or re-discover) their love for learning requires teachers and administrators to join together in the work. Developing a common conceptualization of the term "civic engagement" is an important first step in this process. This common understanding can provide a theoretical and practical civic foundation that will enable all members of the school community to work toward the same goals. This will be especially important as they develop and incorporate not only innovative instruction but the necessary policies to ensure that robust communities of practice for civic engagement flourish across the school.

Civic engagement can be understood as different civic competencies addressing both formal and informal civic practices. Formal civic practices are often the focus of explicit teaching and learning. For example, traditional civic education focuses on developing knowledge in areas such as government processes and structures, the political system, the nature and purposes of constitutions, and voting.

Focusing only on the conventional civic activities is insufficient, however, especially when addressing the social and cognitive development of students' understanding of political, civic, and social responsibility. We have tended to ignore the broader concepts and processes related to civic engagement, such as working with others to solve school and neighborhood problems, understanding people who have different ideas, participating in curriculum-based social movement activities, and developing the skills necessary to understand and address complex cultural issues. Communities of practice in schools help build a wider range of civic skills, attitudes, and behaviors. These also include an array of informal civic practices, such as cultivating healthy normative structures in schools to support students' civic development. Students who have the fewest opportunities to participate in communities of practice are also likely to have the lowest levels of civic capacity (Homana, 2009).

Teachers need to employ instructional practices that move beyond traditional teaching approaches such as lecturing. Opportunities for focused discussion of controversial issues can help students grapple with the social, political, and cultural forces that underlie these issues so that they are better prepared to understand and address these types of problems in society. Service-learning is another powerful approach. Service-learning incorporates academic work with actual school and neighborhood needs to foster student academic success and civic engagement. The connection between communities of practice and high-quality service-learning can serve to actively engage students in learning while developing critical thinking and problem-solving skills. Importantly, it is a way for teachers to become facilitators for student learning. Also, student involvement in activities such as student councils and school newspapers, as well as the arts and theater that promote social imagination (see e.g., Greene, 1995) are excellent for this purpose. Additionally, fostering clusters of communities of practice that involve school engagement, youth and community programs, and museums may help ensure higher academic and civic success for students, as compared to those who do not experience these opportunities.

Finally, achieving the greatest impact on the development of students' civic capacities might best be addressed through consideration of a three-pronged approach. First, though it is incumbent upon teachers and administrators to create the type of school environment that is conducive to communities of practice, it is also necessary that they find ways to encourage students to participate in these learning opportunities. While the classroom is a natural setting for communities of practice, it should not be considered the only venue for the work. Rather, it is important for schools to create an environment that promotes broad and effective participation in the dimensions of communities of practice *throughout* and *across* the school. In this way, students can experience the collective nature of civic learning and engagement. Second, the value of the combined potential positive effects of participation in all communities of practice suggests that schools seriously consider providing a comprehensive range of communities of practice that involve discussion, collaboration, and real-world participation. Given current educational aims, which focus almost exclusively on a narrow range of academic outcomes, this will require refocusing the mission of the school through a set of innovative instructional strategies, as well as agreed-upon policies that promote conscious commitment to communities of practice. This work could focus, for example, on evaluation and possible revision of mission statements; on issues in curriculum and instruction; on the frequency, quality, and type of professional development offered to teachers; and, especially, on the inclusion of all school members, including students, in decision-making processes. Third, and equally important, is support among members of the school community, parents, students, and educators alike, for securing action around the potential positive values and norms associated with communities of practice to promote the development of civic capacities.

Rich and interactive learning experiences can ignite students' passions about civic practices. This chapter has presented a positive notion of the *discourse community of practice*, the *collaborative community of practice*, and the *participatory community of practice* for civic engagement based on healthy norms of behavior, expectations, attitudes, and actions across the school environment. These positive ways of thinking and behavior are nurtured by both the curriculum and the normative structures that shape how members of a school community interact with each other. If we want our young people to engage actively not only in their learning but also in making a difference in society, schools must find ways to promote the creation of communities of practice.

## References

Battistich, V., Solomon, D., Watson, M., & Schaps, E. (1997). Caring school communities. *Educational Psychologist, 32*(3), 137–151.

Billig, S., Root, S., & Jesse, D. (2005). *The impact of participation in service-learning on high school students' civic engagement* (Working Paper No. 33). Retrieved from the Center for Information and Research on Civic Learning and Engagement website: http://www.servicelearningnetwork.org/wp-content/uploads/2014/09/WP33Billig.pdf

Brown, E.L., Powell, E., & Clark, A. (2012). Working on what works: Working with teachers to improve classroom behaviors and relationships. *Educational Psychology in Practice, 28*(1), 19–30.

Cappella, E., Neal, J.W., & Sahu, N. (2012). Children's agreement on classroom social networks: Cross-level predictors in urban elementary schools. *Merrill-Palmer Quarterly, 58*(3), 285–313.

Gifford, C., Watt, P., Clark, W., & Koster, S. (2005). Negotiating participation and power in a school setting: The implementation of active citizenship within the undergraduate sociology curriculum. *Learning and Teaching in the Social Sciences, 2*(3), 175–190.

Greene, M. (1995). *Releasing the imagination: Essays on education, the arts, and social change.* San Francisco, CA: Jossey-Bass.

Hess, D., & Avery, P.G. (2008). Discussion of controversial issues as a form and goal of democratic education. In J. Arthur, I. Davies, & C. Hahn (Eds.), *The SAGE handbook of education for citizenship and democracy* (pp. 506–518). London: Sage Publications.

Homana, G. (2009, December). *Communities of practice for the development of adolescent civic engagement: An empirical study of their correlates in Australia and the United States*. Doctoral dissertation, University of Maryland. Available from ProQuest Dissertations & Theses database (Publication No. UMD10871).

Homana, G., & Passe, J. (2013). Not too hot, not too cold: Social studies in today's middle schools. In J. Passe & P.G. Fitchett (Eds.), *Research on the status of social studies: Views from the field*. Charlotte, NC: Information Age.

Kahne, J., Crow, D., & Lee, N.-J. (2013). Different pedagogy, different politics: High school learning opportunities and youth political engagement. *Political Psychology, 34*(3), 419–441.

Kahne, J., Rodriquez, M., Smith, B., & Thiede, K. (2000). Developing citizens for democracy? Assessing opportunities to learn in Chicago's social studies classrooms. *Theory and Research in Social Education, 28*(3), 311–338.

Kahne, J., & Sporte, S. (2008). Developing citizens: The impact of civic learning opportunities on students' commitment to civic participation. *American Educational Research Journal, 45*(3), 738–766.

Kennedy, K.J., & Mellor, S. (2006). Australian students' civic attitudes as indicators of support for social capital: Learning outcomes for the future. *Educational Psychology, 26*(2), 251–271.

Lave, J., & Wenger, E. (1991). *Situated learning: Legitimate peripheral participation*. Cambridge, UK: Cambridge University Press.

Lave, J., & Wenger, E. (2001). Legitimate peripheral participation in communities of practice. In M. Lea & K. Nicol (Eds.), *Distributed learning: Social and cultural approaches to practice* (pp. 56–63). London: RoutledgeFalmer.

Levinson, B.A.U., & Brantmeier, E.J. (2006). Secondary schools and communities of practice for democratic civic education: Challenges of authority and authenticity. *Theory and Research in Social Education, 34*(3), 324–346.

Ludden, A.B. (2011). Engagement in school and community civic activities in rural adolescents. *Journal of Youth Violence, 40,* 1254–1270.

Postman, N. (1996). *The end of education: Redefining the value of school.* New York: Vintage Books.

Roseth, C.J., Johnson, D.W., & Johnson, R.T. (2008). Promoting early adolescents' achievement and peer relationships: The effects of cooperative, competitive, and individualistic goal structures. *Psychological Bulletin, 134*(2), 223–246.

Torney-Purta, J., Amadeo, J., & Richardson, W.K. (2007). Civic service among youth in Chile, Denmark, England, and the United States. In A.M. McBride & M. Sherraden (Eds.), *Civic service worldwide: Impacts and inquiry* (pp. 95–132). New York: M.E. Sharpe.

Torney-Purta, J., Homana, G., & Barber, C. (2006, April). *Young people's social and political attitudes and communities of practice in four countries.* Paper presented at symposium conducted at the American Educational Research Association Conference, San Francisco, CA.

Torney-Purta, J., & Richardson, W. (2003). Teaching for the meaningful practice of democratic citizenship: Learning from the IEA Civic Education Study in 28 countries. In J. Patrick, G.E. Hamot, and R.S. Leming (Eds.), *Principles and practices of democracy in the education of social studies teachers* (vol. 2, pp. 25–44). Retrieved from http://eric.ed.gov

Urdan, T., & Schoenfelder, E. (2006). Classroom effects on student motivation: Goal structures, social relationships, and competence beliefs. *Journal of School Psychology, 44,* 331–349.

Vygotsky, L. (1986). *Thought and language.* Boston: MIT Press.

Wenger, E. (1998). *Communities of practice: Learning and meaning in school.* New York: Cambridge University Press.

Wenger, E. (2014). *Learning in landscapes of practice: Boundaries, identity and knowledgeability in practice-based learning.* Abington Oxon, UK: Routledge.

Wentzel, K. (1994). Relations of social goal pursuit to social acceptance, classroom behavior, perceived social support. *Journal of Educational Psychology, 86*(2), 173–182.

Wentzel, K. (1997). Student motivation in middle school: The role of perceived pedagogical caring. *Journal of Educational Psychology, 89*(3), 411–419.

Wentzel, K.R. (1998). Social relationships and motivation in middle school: The role of parents, teachers, and peers. *Journal of Educational Psychology, 90*(2), 202–209.

Wentzel, K.R., Barry, C.M., & Caldwell, K.A. (2004). Friendships in middle school: Influences on motivation and school adjustment. *Journal of Educational Psychology, 96*(2), 195–203.

# CHAPTER TEN

# CONNECTING STUDENTS AND COMMUNITIES
## Locally Relevant Texts

KARI DAHLE-HUFF

THERE IS A GROWING trend in the United States to locally source food, labor, and goods. So why not utilize locally relevant texts for students to read as well? A locally relevant text is one that reflects the political climate, culture, language, history, or community in which the school is located. A locally relevant text is grounded in *place-conscious education* (Gruenewald, 2003a), which connects learning sourced from people and organizations in the community to the school curriculum. Teaching with locally relevant texts not only strengthens the bond between schools, community members, and students, but also makes learning more engaging, responsive, and relevant. Locally relevant texts can and do lead to authentic investigations in schools and communities, which in turn engages 21st-century critical thinking skills. According to Demarest (2015), authentic investigations connected to place "can foster higher-order thinking, authentic problem solving, and a cognitive richness that promotes academic achievement" (p. 17). When students read a text about local issues or populations or conduct other investigations, they begin to see value in where they live. Locally relevant texts provide a dynamic curriculum that connects the lived experiences of students to issues in local communities.

## Why Students Resist School

Students are complex human beings, and many factors may cause a student to resist schooling. Students may resist school if a parent is incarcerated, if there is food insecurity, or if they have to change schools because of housing uncertainty. Many such factors cannot be eliminated or even mitigated by schooling, but there are things educators can do to help alleviate the isolation and resistance often experienced by students.

Resistance theory supplies a lens for understanding other reasons why students may push back against schooling practices and against learning. Toshalis (2015) states that "research has made it clear that students will be less likely to resist their educators and schooling experiences when youth are given ample opportunities to learn more about their 'othered' cultural heritage" (pp. 217–218). Locally relevant texts provide such an opportunity for students to learn more about their communities and the places they inhabit, as well as their "othered" cultural heritages, languages, histories, and political and economic structures. For students who are unable to see themselves as present and valued in school, schooling practices become isolating, and this is where resistance begins to find traction. In order to make learning relevant to students' lived experiences and for students to find value in school, they need to experience diversity in the texts not only sanctioned by schools, but authentically taken up as well. .

Bishop (1990) offers a helpful metaphor for what a locally relevant text can provide for students. Texts are like mirrors, windows, or sliding glass doors, and readers need only walk through these doors to "become part of whatever world has been created or re-created by the author" (p. ix). A locally relevant text is a glass door that provides an opportunity for students to learn through exploration and to experience the value of the places they inhabit. Further, a locally relevant text allows students to love learning and school again because they are able to experience value in themselves and their places. As Bishop (1990) eloquently states it:

> When children cannot find themselves reflected in the books they read, or when the images they see are distorted, negative, or

laughable, they learn a powerful lesson about how they are deval-
ued in the society of which they are a part. Our classrooms need
to be places where all the children from all the cultures that make
up the salad bowl of American society can find their mirrors. (p. 1)

This chapter examines the idea of place-conscious education and its
intersection with culturally relevant pedagogy before telling the story of a
teacher who offered her students a locally relevant text to examine their
community—a community where Hmong immigrants were numerous, yet
set apart. Her students were given a good, solid answer if they asked the
question that students often want to ask: "So, what does this have to do
with me?" The locally relevant text the teacher selected made the answer
clear: "It's about *you* and *your* community."

## Place-Conscious Education

Gruenewald (2003a) proposed a pedagogy that juxtaposes critical learning
with place-based education and terms this marriage a place-conscious education (PCE). A main corollary of PCE is to extend pedagogy outward to
the community and to extend learning to incorporate the lived experiences
of students. (This includes culture, history, community, family, politics, and
the ecological environment.) As a formative theorist of PCE, Gruenewald
(2003b) states that PCE aims to work against the isolation from the living
world outside that is found in schooling discourses and practices, and the
increasing placelessness of institutions of education. "Thus extended, pedagogy becomes more relevant to the lived experiences of students and teachers, and accountability is conceptualized so that place matters to educators,
students, and citizens in tangible ways" (Gruenewald, 2003b, p. 620). In
other words, PCE enlists teachers, students, and community members to
incorporate learning with the firsthand experience of local life and in the
social and political processes of understanding and shaping what happens
where they live (Gruenewald, 2003a).

PCE utilizes a critical lens to frame education, pedagogy, and learning
specifically centered on place. Stevenson (2008) asserts that PCE grounds
learning and schooling in the local. But what is meant by "local" or by
"place"? I assert that place encompasses not only the physical surroundings
that our students move through on a day-to-day basis, but also the social

communities and interactions that students value. Place is a nebulous construct because it is individual to each student and to each school. Similarly, Stevenson (2008) suggests that the concept of place needs to be expanded beyond the physical and to include "out-of-school social and virtual sites that serve as alternative texts" (p. 355). For example, a student interested in beekeeping may post comments and pictures on the local beekeeping Facebook page. Place is then conceptualized and understood as a "lens through which young people begin to make sense of themselves and their surroundings. It is where they form relationships and social networks, develop a sense of community, and learn to live with others" (McInerney, Smyth, & Down, 2011, p. 5). Student agency is therefore central to determining what constitutes place and to inclusionary educational practices such as teaching with locally relevant texts.

John Dewey (1916) and other progressives of the early 20th century advocated for incorporating students' experience of particular communities and places into learning, but "the tendency toward centralization and standardization in the broader society marginalized their perspectives and practices they advocated" (Gruenewald & Smith, 2010, p. 1). The push toward centralization and standardization is again prominent in education, and PCE is an antithesis to standardization of curriculum. PCE is an approach that connects learning with student knowledge, lived experiences, and place, but also includes addressing standards that are mandated in education. It is the meeting of PCE and locally relevant texts that connects standards and rigorous learning with local knowledge, while simultaneously making school more connected to students' lived experiences and place. High standards for learning are actually enhanced by locally relevant texts and PCE because students' engagement and motivation increases with a connection between their lives outside of school and what they are learning. This, in turn, engages 21st-century critical thinking skills with critical reading and writing. Gruenewald (2003b) proposes that a place-conscious framework measuring student achievement can assess learning in relation to the pedagogical impact of place in and outside of school.

The challenge for educators is to recognize that no matter where they are—no matter the neighborhood—math, science, literature, art, history, and culture surround them and their schools (Sobel, 2004; Tolbert & Theobald, 2006). Resources for learning abound in every community, and often these resources are excluded from traditional schooling because they are not on standardized tests. It is when these curricular resources are left out that school becomes sterile and students lose sight of themselves in the curriculum.

> The beauty of place-based education is that it cannot only serve as a vehicle for learning school subjects, but also give students an opportunity to develop inter- and intrapersonal intelligence, as they work with one another and discover something about the hardships they share living in America's passed-over urban places. (Tolbert & Theobald, 2006, p. 274)

A connection between students' lived experiences and learning is not a new idea; however, what PCE does is frame a more reciprocal relationship between community and school. According to Moll, Amanti, Neff, and Gonzalez (1992), students' "funds of knowledge" are a connection to community and things local that students already have when they enter schools. However, this connection presents only one side of a dialogic relationship in learning: it accounts for the knowledge that students bring to learning but does not reflect the resources for learning found locally, or how learning is connected to community through locally relevant texts. PCE accounts for students' "funds of knowledge" while simultaneously utilizing local resources such as places, texts, and people as instructional resources. PCE further uses experiential learning methods to increase skills and attitudes in group dynamics, human relations, and community building to strengthen already existing curricula (PEEC, 2010; Gruenewald & Smith, 2010).

By choosing a locally relevant text that directly connects to the community, teachers are engaging students in a firsthand experience of learning about the local, while critically thinking about the political processes that shape what happens there. This is essential PCE. Using texts connected to local communities and cultures, students are able to (1) see their lived experiences in the curriculum as a mirror, window, or sliding glass door; (2) experience a sense of value in the places they occupy; and (3) engage in a new localism and become active community participants. Further, Gruenewald (2003a) asks educators to engage critically with their community and advocates that the texts students and teachers explore reflect the "images of their own concrete, situated experiences with the world" (p. 5).

## The Crossroads of Place-Conscious Education
## and Culturally Relevant Pedagogy

Gloria Ladson-Billings (1995) defined culturally relevant pedagogy as:

> a pedagogy of opposition...not unlike critical pedagogy but specifi-
> cally committed to collective, not merely individual, empowerment.
> Culturally relevant pedagogy rests on three criteria or propositions:
> (a) students must experience academic success; (b) students must
> develop and/or maintain cultural competence; and (c) students
> must develop a critical consciousness through which they challenge
> the status quo of the current social order. (p. 160)

Critical pedagogy provides an overarching framework for connecting
place-conscious pedagogy and culturally relevant pedagogy. At the cross-
roads of this framework are locally relevant texts, which combine critical
examinations of place and culture into learning that is both conscious and
relevant.

Learning that is framed through a culturally relevant pedagogical lens
and connected to place-conscious education naturally leads to a selection of
locally relevant texts and learning resources.

### Community Reflected in the Text

In a large Midwestern city, one teacher chose to take up a locally relevant
text with her students that reflected the experiences of a large immigrant
community there. The book *Tangled Threads: A Hmong Girl's Story* (2003),
by Pegi Dietz Shea, was read by a 7th-grade class, and through critical discussions the students began to explore the Hmong immigrant experience
in their own community. Although there were no Hmong students in this
class, there were Hmong students in the school, and this metropolitan area
has the largest Hmong population outside of Vietnam. Choosing a text that
is a window to this community is important because it offers students the
opportunity to become familiar with community members.

The teacher, Anne (a pseudonym), made a deliberate choice to use this
text in her classroom, as she communicated to me through personal corre-
spondence. She stated:

I was looking for a fictional novel or memoir detailing the journey
of the Hmong from Laos to the US that would be appropriate for
middle school aged students since we have such a high population
of Hmong residents. I didn't want that narrative ignored and not
represented in my curriculum and in school in general.

Greenwood (2013) supports Anne's reasoning by suggesting that PCE can
build a "conceptual framework that explicitly critiques problematic ends
of schooling and that articulates educational purposes and possibilities that
are woefully neglected in the discourse of schooling" (p. 95). Along with the
Hmong narrative, Anne provided contextual information about this locally
relevant text, including information on the Vietnam War and the role of
Hmong. During critical class discussions, Anne covered such difficult topics with students as chemical weapons used in war, life in refugee camps,
and relationships. Specifically, the relationship between family members
throughout their immigration experience was discussed, particularly the
changes in relationships that occurred. By studying this fictional Hmong
narrative, Anne provided space for her students to understand their own
community more deeply and how intertwined people are in the places they
live. She stated:

I felt that the Hmong immigration story was a vital one to have as
part of a larger theme of identity. The book appears to be well researched and students respond to it well, and it is a great leaping off
place for me to be able to talk about history, politics, war, immigration, cultural appropriation, etc. But my major issue with it is that it
is written by a white American woman and not from someone from
the Hmong culture who could speak with an authentic voice. I'm
still searching for that book! There are a few narratives but not one
that I've found that is appropriate for this age level.

Bishop (1990) touches on the topic of cultural authenticity and the need
for texts that will help students understand the multicultural nature of the
world they live in, the places they occupy in it, and their connections to others (p. 1). Authenticity in texts not only adds to the richness of reading but
also identifies uniqueness found in characters of all sorts. The frustration

expressed by the teacher above is evident and understandable as she continues to search for authentic texts documenting the Hmong immigrant experience.

### Critical Reading and Writing
Smith (2002) suggests that using the critical lens of PCE and locally relevant texts provides a pathway to making the "boundaries between schools and their environs more permeable by directing at least part of students' school experiences to local phenomena ranging from culture and politics to environmental concerns and the economy" (p. 190). Anne directed her students' school experiences toward local culture and history through her text choice and discussions:

> While reading, the biggest theme we talk through is "thread." Before reading, we talk through a brief history of the Hmong people, from 5000 B.C. up through the Vietnam War and today. We touch on the role of the U.S. in armed conflicts outside the U.S., immigration, etc., as well. I try to both let the novel guide the discussion along with identifying themes that students may find relevant to their lives—welfare, public assistance, friendships, child-adult conflict—and I always try to bring current events, race/privilege, and politics into the discussion to help them be more aware of how the world around them works.

At the end of the unit, before students began their projects on topics related to the book, Anne showed a documentary on the Hmong to give students more ideas and information. She made deliberate connections to local community members while teaching this unit. She invited a local Hmong hip-hop artist to perform and share his tattoos of Pa'ndau, which is a traditional form of Hmong artwork. This artist spoke to the students about the Pa'ndau and their historical and present symbolism. Pa'ndau is art that is stitched onto cloth and tells a story or records the Hmong people's history. Pa'ndau, or flower cloth, is similar to a quilt, but this cloth has the history of the Hmong people stitched onto it, and it is revered (Lee, 1996).

Understanding the symbolism of Hmong artwork is one example of critical reading with a locally relevant text. Another example of a critical reading with a text is exploring the cultural and historical references, such as stories shared within a culture. According to Anne:

> I've also relatively recently discovered the Hmong origin story, which I share with students, and I continue to try to find speakers, interviews, videos, etc. of voices that represent the Hmong in today's world. I think it is really important to do that explicitly and to not be non-specific. I also work really hard to remind students that my understanding of the Hmong culture, of the story, etc. comes filtered through my lens as a privileged white American woman and invite them to examine their own filters and lenses, and those of the author.

Again, the importance of the critical lens is stressed with this locally relevant text, and Anne deliberately models inward examination for students so that the class is able to unpack the lenses that they themselves use. This pedagogy exemplifies PCE in that the teacher is connecting learning to the community outside of school while encouraging students to use a critical lens to heighten the learning experience. Especially important is the deep exploration of privilege and unpacking individual filters. Anne deliberately engineered discussions in her class that explored these topics and gave students a scaffold and safe learning environment to take up these complicated issues. She created a final project for this locally relevant text in which students researched and then made a presentation on the Hmong culture or some other theme found in the book. Students were able to deepen their understanding but also make their learning relevant to their own interests. Students, through these critical conversations and their final projects exploring the Hmong culture, were able to connect their learning to their community.

An example of a student project that used locally relevant texts to explore the community was an interview project put together by Eva. Eva created a final paper that explored Hmong art in the community. For this project Eva researched three well-known Hmong artists living in the community—Kao Lee Thao, Mai C. Vang, and Tou Yia Xiong. These artists did not always explicitly include traditional Hmong symbols in their artwork (the symbols discussed in class), but sometimes they did. Not only did Eva include local Hmong artists in her paper, but her research also led her to include an art professor at a local college and an art teacher at another local high school. Both of these professionals were able to discuss Hmong art and the Hmong community. It is local resources such as these that exemplify PCE and the importance of using locally relevant texts. Eva herself best describes the pedagogical impact of such a research project: "That was my paper on Hmong artists in MN, the artists I wrote about don't do traditional hmong [*sic*] art, but incorporate it in their art sometimes. I hope you learned about local hmong [*sic*] artists and go check out some of their art sometime." Eva was able to connect her own interest in art to what she had read in school and then find members of the community who would share their own expert knowledge. When schooling makes these connections between school and community, learning is more meaningful and relevant.

Anne's pedagogy of place and use of locally relevant texts, as described through her own narrative, connects what she teaches in class not only to students' lived experiences but also to the local. It is through this pedagogy of place that Anne is taking up the characteristics of PCE—especially a critical examination of topics covered in class. Gruenewald (2003a) states:

> Given the cultural complexity of decolonizing and reinhabiting places, especially in an educational climate that is increasingly focused on quantitative, paper-and-pencil outcomes at the expense of any conversation about what it means to live well in a place, developing a movement for critical, place-based educational practices is a difficult proposition. (p. 11)

Place and new localism may be difficult propositions; however, they are extremely useful to students in developing a sense of value in where they live and what they learn.

## Engaging Students with Locally Relevant Texts

Students who are able to see their lived experiences or the communities in which they live reflected in what they are learning are simultaneously engaging in relevant and responsive learning. An authentic voice in text choice is an important consideration for teachers, as Anne mentions. Books can be, variously, windows, mirrors, or sliding glass doors for students to explore, and educators need to be conscious of authenticity in order for students to experience a sense of value in the places they occupy. When learning inside the classroom connects to the larger community outside the school, students are able to better understand and participate in community. In turn, they learn how to become an engaged citizenry, one of the foundational pillars of a democracy. Demarest (2015) states that

> when the work is truly embedded in the community, and reflects the issues that face society, the answers will not be confined to the classroom. Big issues are dealt with, real problems solved, and authentic partnerships forged. Students become problem solvers, civic agents, community leaders, team members. (p. 98)

The use of local authors and writers is an important path for "embedding the work," which connects learning to the local. Further, using locally relevant texts allows students to see value in the places in which they live, and to engage in localism by being active in the community. Locally relevant texts provide a vehicle for making the walls of the school more permeable, allowing the local community to participate actively with students and learning. The use of locally relevant texts creates learning environments that are conducive to critical reading and writing that is culturally and socially relevant. Finally, it has the potential to ignite a love of school in students who may have felt left out.

## References

Bishop, R.S. (1990). Mirrors, windows, and sliding glass doors. *Perspectives, 1*(3), ix–xi.

Demarest, A.B. (2015). *Place-based curriculum design: Exceeding standards through local investigations*. New York: Routledge.

Dewey, J. (1916). *Democracy and education: An introduction to the philosophy of education*. New York: Macmillan.

Greenwood, D. (2013). A critical theory of place-conscious education. In R.B. Stevenson, M. Brody, J. Dillon, & A.E.J. Wals (Eds.), *International handbook on environmental education* (pp. 93–100). New York: Routledge.

Gruenewald, D.A. (2003a). The best of both worlds: A critical pedagogy of place. *Educational Researcher, 32*(4), 3–12.

Gruenewald, D.A. (2003b). Foundations of place: A multidisciplinary framework for place-conscious education. *American Educational Research Journal, 40*(3), 619–654.

Gruenewald, D.A., & Smith, G.A. (2010). Introduction: Making room for the local. In D. Gruenewald & G. Smith (Eds.), *Place-based education in the global age* (pp. xiii–xxiii). New York: Routledge.

Ladson-Billings, G. (1995). But that's just good teaching! The case for culturally relevant pedagogy. *Theory into Practice, 34*(3), 159–165. Retrieved from http://www.jstor.org.proxybl.lib.montana.edu/stable/1476635

Lee, J.H. (1996, June 23). On Hmong quilt, every stitch holds years of history and culture. *Los Angeles Times*. Retrieved from http://articles.latimes .com/1996-06-23/local/me-17831_1_hmong-history

McInerney, P., Smyth, J., & Down, B. (2011). Coming to a place near you: The politics and possibilities of a critical pedagogy of place-based education. *Asian-Pacific Journal of Teacher Education, 39*(1), 3–16.

Moll, L., Amanti, C., Neff, D., & Gonzalez, N. (1992). Funds of knowledge for teaching: Using a qualitative approach to connect homes and classrooms. *Theory into Practice, 31*(2), 132–141.

Place-Based Education Evaluation Collaborative (PEEC). (2010). *The benefits of place-based education: A report from the Place-Based Education Evaluation Collaborative*. Retrieved from http://www.peecworks.org/ PEEC/Benefits_of_PBE-PEEC_2008_web.pdf

Shea, P.D. (2003). *Tangled threads: A Hmong girl's story*. New York: Clarion.

Smith, G.A. (2002). Place-based education: Learning to be where we are. *Phi Delta Kappan, 83*(8), 584–594.

Sobel, D. (2004). *Place-based education: Connecting classrooms and communities*. Great Barrington, MA: The Orion Society.

Somerville, M.J. (2010). A place pedagogy for "global contemporaneity." *Educational Philosophy and Theory, 42*(3), 326–344.

Stevenson, R.B. (2008). A critical pedagogy of place and the critical place(s) of pedagogy. *Environmental Education Research, 14*(3), 353–360.

Tolbert, L., & Theobald, P. (2006). Finding their place in the community: Urban education outside of the classroom. *Childhood Education, 82*(5), 271–274.

Toshalis, E. (2015). *Make me! Understanding and engaging student resistance in school.* Cambridge, MA: Harvard Education Press.

# CHAPTER ELEVEN

# "A TOOLBOX FOR WORKING ..."

## The Disappearance of Developmentally Appropriate Practices

MEGAN HALLISSEY

### Developmentally Appropriate Practice

THE NATIONAL ASSOCIATION FOR the Education of Young Children (NAEYC) is an organization that increases public understanding of children's development, with a specific focus on early childhood—birth through age eight. It promotes high-quality early learning for young children by connecting early childhood practice, policy, and research (NAEYC, 2015). Thirty years ago, NAEYC published a position statement that would become widely known as developmentally appropriate practices (DAP) for educators serving children from birth through age eight (Bredekamp, 1987). It was a synopsis of what educators had learned over the last two centuries including, among other things, ideas about children being active learners, an emphasis on discovery and exploration, opportunities for problem-solving and critical thinking skills, the inclusion of hands-on cooperative learning projects, and the cultivation of lifelong learning skills (Hallissey, 2017).

Established from theory, research, and literature, developmentally appropriate practices require meeting children where they are—based on knowledge rather than on assumptions about how children learn and develop (Copple & Bredekamp, 2009). DAP's emphasis is on instruction that is appropriate to the age and developmental stages of children, educating all of a child's developmental domains and addressing the interrelatedness among them. The idea behind DAP is to align teaching strategies with current research about children's development and learning capabilities, while also accounting for children's ages, experiences, abilities, and interests (Copple, Bredekamp, Koralek, & Charner, 2014).

Research in neuroscience also supports developmentally appropriate practices and argues that the early childhood years are critical to growth and development. During this time, cognitive capacities in young children increase due to lateralization, allowing the two hemispheres of the brain to begin functioning more efficiently (Harris, 1986). This is also the most sensitive period for brain development, a time in which activating multiple pathways promotes rapid brain growth (Konecki & Schiller, 2003). Activities such as authentic, hands-on learning that engage multiple senses simultaneously stimulate this brain growth as thousands of neural circuit connectors are made stronger (Hallissey, 2017). Without such stimulation, these connectors are eliminated. Once they are lost, they do not return, making early experiences critical to the construction, development, and function of the brain (Calder, 2014).

For children ages five to seven, in particular, the brain is especially responsive to stimulation. Authentic and experiential learning, found in developmentally appropriate practices, can help sculpt regions of the brain (Copple & Bredekamp, 2009). Such practices mold the frontal lobes as well (areas devoted to regulating thought and action) and help to facilitate reasoning, problem-solving, and emotional self-regulation (Copple et al., 2014). Therefore, teaching approaches and learning experiences grounded in developmentally appropriate practices help create and maintain more of the neuron pathways of the brain. Yet despite extensive evidence from brain research and developmental science about the importance of developmentally appropriate practices, the latter are rarely found in schools today and become nonexistent as children progress through grade levels (Hallissey, 2017).

## Classroom Research in Schools

The decline of these best teaching and learning practices becomes evident when one spends extended periods of time in a school setting. Over the past five years, I have observed and interviewed key stakeholders involved with early childhood education—children, parents, early childhood and elementary certified teachers, principals, and supervisors. My own familiarity with school practices as a former teacher, administrator, and kindergarten mother has helped shape my perspective and research in this area. My qualitative and quantitative research studies have focused on six distinct areas: (1) the recognition and utilization of instructional practices to enhance and support early childhood learning in elementary schools; (2) the application of child development principles in the design of curriculum content within elementary schools; (3) the identification of early learning assessment strategies used to classify, address, and evaluate a child's learning and development in elementary schools; (4) the defining of potential knowledge gaps for both elementary teachers and principals regarding early childhood learning; (5) the examination of external factors that influence and/or prevent developmentally appropriate practices from occurring; and (6) the construction of early childhood concepts and how they may influence and shape leadership decisions. The contextual examples offered in real-life situations reflect the need to establish developmentally appropriate practices in elementary-level classrooms.

A summary of my research has been provided along with participants' direct quotes to help highlight specific and critical areas of concern. I have also made a concerted effort to include the voices of children, as most research tends to report from the top down, often ignoring the perspectives of children altogether (Harrist, Thompson, & Norris, 2007). Instead of asking for children's ideas and input, researchers often impose adult ideas on what they *believe* children think or feel (Hallissey, 2017). The children's responses from these different research studies exemplify how they feel and their desire for more interactive learning. These responses also illustrate the ways in which the developmental needs of children are not being met.

### The Absence of Play

The absence of play inside classrooms was undisputed by all stakeholders—principals, teachers, parents, and even children. Interviews with principals and teachers reflected their minimal knowledge about the applicability and practicality of play, specifically for the 1st, 2nd, and 3rd grades. One elementary school principal admitted that he struggled in this area: "Maybe it's because I've never seen it" (Hallissey, 2017, p. 111). A 1st-grade teacher had similar thoughts, stating: "I wouldn't even know how to go about playing" (p. 111). The lack of knowledge about early childhood appeared to influence instructional strategies within a classroom, as neither the teacher nor the principal claimed to know how to incorporate play as a learning medium.

In another school, the lack of play was noticed by the children. As little Sammy told me disappointedly, "I have a Superhero Cape that I play with a lot. But I'm not supposed to bring a Superhero Cape here...it's against school rules." In a subsequent conversation, I asked the kindergarten teacher whether she had costumes for dramatic play or props for role-playing. She stated, "Do you mean like a dress-up center?" When a parent was asked about her level of comfort with the teacher's knowledge, she stated, "I defer to the teacher." But classroom instruction might suggest otherwise, as developmentally appropriate practices didn't seem to occur, indicating a lack of expertise and foundational knowledge. Sammy's mother corroborated these findings, explaining, "I don't think they have many chances to use their imagination because he'll get home and it's like all built up—he wants to play with army guys for two hours. He's just gotta get it out!"

The misconception that children don't learn through play or the need to distinguish between "learning through play" and "learning academic content" appears to grow stronger as children progress through school (Hallissey, 2017). However, studies in early childhood classrooms identify how beneficial child-directed play can be as it relates to problem-solving, literacy, mathematics, and social-emotional growth (Anderson, Spainhower, & Sharp, 2014). This research suggests that a lack of play in elementary classrooms might even be inhibiting student growth and development in both cognitive and social-emotional areas. One mother recalled discussing kindergarten with her daughter, who was complaining about the lack of play in school. "'You're going to have to sit and do worksheets,' I told her. It's not just play. You are not going to get the ponies out." When the principal was asked about the lack of play allowed in classrooms, she admitted feeling torn about pushing "academic" learning at such an early age. "It's hard to know what the balance is—wanting them to have that good academic foundation, but to the point of frustration? Are we asking them to do things that their brains may not be ready to do?"

## Predetermined Curriculum and Cookie-Cutter Teaching

National professional standards for both teachers (Teacher Leadership Exploratory Consortium, 2011) and educational administrators (National Policy Board for Educational Administration, 2015) highlight and require that instructional strategies be both differentiated and personalized for students. However, similar instructional methods and pre-determined curricula that are often found in schools today rarely seem to address the needs of individual students. One assistant principal referred to it as "cookie cutter teaching" and hoped that, despite specific mandates, the "prescribed curriculum" was still varied within a classroom (Hallissey, 2017, p. 132). But most times instructional strategies weren't varied and failed to account both for the different rates of children's development and for the different ways children learn (Hallissey, 2017). Identical teaching strategies and identical curriculum content across grade levels appeared to be expected for continuity so that "one would see the exact same information being taught in every single class in that grade level," as one principal explained (Hallissey, 2017, p. 191). But this is not reflective of early childhood pedagogy, which recognizes that "development and learning proceed at varying rates from child to child, as well as at uneven rates across different areas" (Copple & Bredekamp, 2009, p. 13). Teaching requires more than covering the curriculum. It requires teachers who can "present critical ideas in powerful ways and systematically organize a learning process that builds on students' prior knowledge and addresses their different needs" (Darling-Hammond, 1999, p. 29).

Other instructional practices that are often favored in elementary schools not only contradict early childhood pedagogy (Copple & Bredekamp, 2009), but may be counterproductive when accounting for children's learning (Institute of Medicine [IOM] & National Research Council [NRC], 2015). For example, one study took 448 3rd-grade students and randomly assigned them to an individualized instructional intervention or a vocabulary intervention that was not individualized (Conner et al., 2011). They found that those students who received individualized instruction made greater gains on a standardized assessment of reading comprehension (Conner et al., 2011). But such individualized instruction was not apparent in any of the schools or classrooms I visited. One kindergarten teacher reported that her class listened to the Color Song every day, for the last forty days. Requiring students to sit still on a rug and listen, the "Color Song" identified items that were of similar color and spelled out the word (i.e., apple, firetruck, ambulance lights, etc.).

Yet none of the children I interviewed correctly spelled the colors. As one kindergartener explained, "We listen to it every day...we do it when it's almost time to leave. I don't know how to spell purple, but D-L-U-E spells blue."

## Educating Holistically

Educating the whole child is a critical component of developmentally appropriate practices (Copple et al., 2014). This means addressing all the domains of learning, including physical, social/emotional, and cognitive. Creativity is another critical aspect that should be included in the education of the whole child, yet minimal opportunities to be creative in schools exist (Hallissey, 2017). Art, for example, is frequently eliminated from the curriculum as a result of budgetary constraints. Teachers and principals confirm that art is essentially nonexistent in most classrooms, even though educators often declare that they hold art and creativity in high regard (Hallissey, 2017).

When art is a component of classroom instruction, it is minimal at best, often using template art with predetermined materials and designs. When one kindergarten teacher was asked whether she allowed for open-ended art projects in her classroom, her response was, "Like allow them to create whatever they want? No." (Hallissey, 2017, p. 164). During the observation of a 2nd-grade classroom, the teacher had her students decorate a plastic cup with four predetermined colors. Students were to use their fingertips to place polka-dots on the outside of the cup, creating a Mother's Day vase. One boy decided to make stripes instead, and the teacher penalized him upon this discovery. When asked about this instructional choice, the teacher stated, "It looks better with polka dots...and he didn't follow directions." The student was forbidden to participate in any classroom celebrations occurring the next day, the school's monthly reward, and was not allowed to give the "vase" to his mother (Hallissey, 2017).

Creativity is an essential component of divergent thinking. According to one study conducted by Land and Jarman (1992), creativity greatly diminishes as people progress through school. When kindergarten students were asked how many uses they could find for a paper clip, 98% scored at the genius level in divergent thinking. When these same students were 10 years old, only 32% of them were at this level, and by age 15, only 10% made the cut. When 200,000 adults were given the same test, only 2% tested at the genius level (Land & Jarman, 1992). Perhaps more creativity is warranted when designing the scope and sequence of school curriculum, especially as it relates to the development of the whole child.

Educating holistically also seems to diminish as children progress through grade levels. In particular, children in the elementary grades appear to face specific challenges, due to the pressures placed on educators to narrow perceived achievement gaps, improve their academic performance in different subject areas, and increase their scores on accountability tests (Hallissey, 2017). As one five-year-old boy explained to me, "I spend a lot of time at my desk." Requirements to meet all of the grade-level standards by the end of the school year and preparation for state testing appear to be the primary objectives in schools. As one principal admitted, "We start typing in Kindergarten because if you can't type, you can't finish the standardized test."

Analyses of current trends in schools indicate that testing mandates are becoming more and more evident in the early elementary grades, which supersedes the importance of developmentally appropriate practices within a classroom (Hallissey, 2017). But studies also indicate this is not what is best for children.

Teachers describe the pressure to cover all of the curriculum as "a little daunting," and felt sometimes the quality of the child's education was sacrificed (Hallissey, 2017). As a result, project-based learning inside school classrooms also seems minimal at best. For example, during one kindergarten classroom observation, children did not even have an opportunity to touch the soil when planting a flower because of time constraints. After the teacher placed a Dixie cup on each of the 21 desks, she went around and put a seed, a cup of soil, and water in each. The children were only allowed to observe their teacher "because there isn't enough time to have them do it." This instructional practice fails to meet the social, emotional, and physical needs of the students and does not reflect (or account for) knowledge of child learning and development.

As one 3rd-grade teacher stated, "It's where the child isn't a component of the instruction anymore" (Hallissey, 2017, p. 172). Sacrificing project-based learning and minimizing student engagement in hopes of increasing test scores was also expressed by the kindergarten students: "We didn't have tool boxes in pre-K," one boy explained. Showing me his pencil box, he elaborated further: "See? It's a box full of your tools for working."

## Negative Learning Environments

After attending only six days of kindergarten, a six-year-old girl began to cry softly, saying, "I don't want my stick moved, Mommy!" The "stick" she was referring to was an individualized popsicle stick that children were required to move up or down on a makeshift traffic light in her new kindergarten class-room. It is a form of classroom management frequently utilized in many ele-mentary classrooms as a way to regulate student behavior, and it does not align with early childhood principles. Additionally, it is an ineffective strategy, since it rarely changes the behavior of child; instead it merely shames him/her while causing other children (without discipline issues) to have a lot of unnecessary anxiety (Hallissey, 2017). However, many administrators don't recognize this classroom management strategy as being inappropriate for elementary children.

Additionally, many school administrators may not recognize negative learning environments or understand the implications these environments may have on children. During one classroom observation, a kindergarten teacher finger-snapped at the children to get their attention or to make them be quiet. This occurred 19 times in a 15-minute period, but the principal did not notice or remark on this. During the same observation, the teacher snatched a child's paper away because his picture "was too scribbly," as the child had taken a pencil and scribbled from left to right several times to make his idea of "trash," indicating what the Earth would look like with-out recycling. Again, this instructional choice went unnoticed by the princi-pal. When the teacher was asked about the incident, she explained that the child's work was too messy (Hallissey, 2017).

A core principle of developmentally appropriate practices is founded on positive guidance and supportive learning environments. As children pro-gress through elementary schools, these practices begin to diminish rapidly (Hallissey, 2017). A Gallup poll surveyed 1,951 principals regarding school recess. Results indicated that 97% believed recess positively impacted stu-dents' social well-being, but 77% took away recess as punishment—a devel-opmentally inappropriate strategy (Robert Wood Johnson Foundation, 2010). One parent seemed unsure about the nature of withholding recess as punishment. She reported that the teacher, who often works in an adminis-trative capacity, has her child sit out of recess often. "I know he has to sit out five minutes of recess if he doesn't get his journal signed. That seems a little strict for kindergarten."

Research outlines the critical components of both guidance and positive learning environments for children from birth through age eight. For exam-ple, Milkie and Warner (2011) assessed how the classroom learning envi-ronment affects children's emotional and behavioral problems and found that in a nationally representative sample of 1st-graders ($N = 10,700$), children in more negative environments exhibited more learning, externalizing, interpersonal, and internalizing problems. Another study also indicated that punishment and ridicule contributed to children feeling unsafe in the classrooms, and could eventually create academic consequences such as poor test scores (Lacoe, 2016). Emphasizing the need for guidance strategies and facilitation—rather than telling a child "No!"—promotes a child's learning, growth, and development. The examples offered indicate the lack of developmentally appropriate practices and exemplify the importance of creating a positive educational learning environment for young children.

### Identifying Gaps in Knowledge about Early Childhood

When analyzing the difference between instructional practices in elementary classrooms and developmentally appropriate practices, there is more than a disparity. If one explores this disconnect further, several contributing factors begin to emerge. For example, research indicates that principals do not have adequate training, experience, or knowledge of children's developmental readiness and interests (Hallissey, 2017). To date, most principal preparatory programs do not require classes in child development or early childhood curriculum and pedagogy (Brown, Squires, Connors-Tadros, & Horowitz, 2014; IOM & NRC, 2015). The majority of elementary school administrators do not have experience teaching early childhood grade levels, either (Hallissey, 2017; Mead, 2011; Szekely, 2013) and have a minimal understanding of how to design, implement, and evaluate programs for young children (Bornfreund, 2012; Göncü, Main, Perone, & Tozer, 2012; Kostelnik & Grady, 2009). As one pre-K to 8th-grade school principal stated:

> I think it would have done me a world of good as a secondary ed candidate undergrad student to spend some time in a first and second grade classroom because all of my time was spent in the secondary classrooms. But actually getting to spend time in those classrooms— that would have been helpful. (Hallissey, 2017, p. 137)

Research indicates that discrepancies exist in preservice teacher training as well. Studies show that many elementary teachers receive little or no training in developmentally appropriate practices for early elementary grades, in contrast to their early childhood–licensed peers (Hallissey, 2017).

One elementary-certified kindergarten teacher explained, "when children get 'free choice' and get 'redirected' [it] sometimes makes my job harder because they come in thinking Kindergarten is that way." She further elaborates, acknowledging, "I *will* tell them, 'No, you can't do that and you *do* have to finish what I ask you to do.'" Preservice training for elementary education majors often focuses on content rather than instructional practices that support how children learn; further, they may fail to address ideas such as child development and instructional practices that support student learning. As one 3rd-grade teacher stated, "I don't know exactly what developmental domains are so I don't really know if I could accurately account for addressing those" (Hallissey, 2017, p. 142).

State certification regulations may also prevent developmentally appropriate practices from taking place in classrooms. For example, early childhood–licensed teachers are generally more restricted in the grade levels they can teach. Although they are more versed in developmentally appropriate practices, developmental growth, and the needs of an individual child, they are rarely hired to teach in elementary schools (Bornfreund, 2011). In a recent study of four elementary schools, only two of 74 teachers were early childhood licensed, indicating a trend in principals' hiring practices (Hallissey, 2017). State licensure generally offers a greater grade span for elementary-licensed teachers than their early childhood counterparts. As a result, administrators have greater flexibility with an elementary-licensed teacher should student enrollment vary.

What constitutes early childhood compounds the problem further. Often people misconstrue what age group is included in early childhood, dismissing it as only pre-kindergarten and kindergarten (Hallissey, 2017). When they think this way, educators often lump all elementary grades together, failing to recognize specific developmental needs of the younger children. As children progress through the elementary grade levels, developmentally appropriate practices become scarce. Although guidelines vary by state, the National Association of the Education of Young Children defines early childhood as birth through age eight. To that end, the need to distinguish early elementary grade levels (K–3rd grade) from upper elementary grade levels (4th–5th grades) becomes imperative, illustrating the need for unique instructional practices, curriculum content, and assessment strategies specific to this age group in order to promote optimal growth and development (Hallissey, 2017).

## A Needed Revival

In the late 1800s, Johann Heinrich Pestalozzi recognized children as active learners who had their own interests, needs, minds, and personalities (Krusi, Karst, Spiegle, & Korzenik, 1875). At a time when children were to be seen and not heard, this idea became revolutionary. G. Stanley Hall initiated the Child Movement, which stressed the importance of early childhood years and encompassed a new body of research that identified children's learning as being inherently different from the learning of adults, therefore requiring different instructional approaches (Rudnitski, 1995). Friedrich Fröbel, often thought of as the creator of kindergarten, believed creative work and play were fundamental principles and believed in the education of the whole child, respecting children's energy and spontaneous creativity (Hill, 1908). Maria Montessori recognized the need for children to be able to work at their own pace and self-select their own tasks (Montessori, 1966). John Dewey and Patty Hill believed children should learn through inquiry and discovery and offered children opportunities to construct with materials and engage in artistic expression (Hill, 1913). These were just a few individuals who were instrumental in reshaping the educational system to promote the learning needs and developmental growth of children.

Unfortunately, this focus has become lost in a sea of high-stakes testing mandates and pressure to show student growth and financial incentives from both state and federal entities to do so. One teacher, referring to the lack of time, stated: "It's bell-to-bell academics now." One-shot assessments are not comprehensive enough to offer valid and reliable information and do not align with developmentally appropriate practices for this age group. But do children even notice the impact to produce successful results? Of the 46 pre-K, kindergartners, and 1st-graders I interviewed, all of the students reported loving school and not disliking any aspect of it. Unfortunately, this enthusiasm dwindled tremendously as children aged. When 60 2nd-graders were asked about school, two out of every three students reported they "hated learning," saying that school was "boring," there was "too much homework," and it "took away from play time." Additionally, their dislike for a particular subject was primarily based on the grades they received. As one 2nd-grader stated, "I like Math the least because I always get bad grades in it." Both 2nd- and 3rd-grade students indicated how much they hated tests—content area tests, preparation for state testing, and the state standardized test itself. Teachers reported that in the 2nd grade, students were subjected to a lot of test preparation and in 3rd grade, high-stakes state testing began (officially being reported). As one 3rd-grader expressed it, "I don't like tests, and I don't like the pressure that makes me feel I have to get it right."

With an increased understanding of child development, educators could create positive learning environments and instructional strategies that are more aligned with developmentally appropriate practices so they can better support early elementary–age children. Instead of confining children to desks, educators could grant them the freedom to move around the classroom and collaborate with their peers. Developmentally appropriate practices recognize that group work can cultivate and foster genuine social cooperation and even enhance understanding of topics (Copple et al., 2014; Hill, 1913). Educators could use children's genuine interest in topics and allow for creative self-expression instead of using a dictated, regimented, and predetermined set of materials. Research in developmentally appropriate practices indicates that children's attention span greatly increases when given an opportunity to learn something they are interested in, rather than content directed by a teacher (Copple & Bredekamp, 2009). Rather than teacher-directed instruction, educators should allow for more child-centered democratic discussions to transpire, giving students ownership and sparking their interest. Instructional strategies that guide, encourage, and cultivate children's exploration, rather than telling students what they should or shouldn't do, are also extremely beneficial. Educators could also create more hands-on learning and increase their fundraising to create more student field trips so that children have more experiential opportunities to touch objects in authentic, real settings. Finally, developmentally appropriate practices teach about authentic assessments—that is, assessments that capture the totality of a child's understanding about a particular concept—rather than rigid assessments that come as pre-packaged tests. Teachers should use different and varied assessment tools to gather a more comprehensive picture of a student's growth and to identify areas of challenge.

Perhaps educators should take notes from past educational crusaders and, like those crusaders, begin to advocate for children—advocate for their interests, abilities, and developmental needs. Perhaps educators should also advocate for change in school classroom structures and start meeting children where they are developmentally, with institutional designs that truly reflect how children learn. After all, as John Dewey eloquently noted over 100 years ago, "the quality of mental process, not the production of correct answers, is the measure of educative growth" (Dewey, 1916).

## References

Anderson, G.T., Spainhower, A.R., & Sharp, A.C. (2014). "Where do the bears go?" The value of child-directed play. *YC: Young Children*, 69(2), 8.

Bornfreund, L. (2011). *Getting in sync: Revamping licensing and preparation for teachers in pre-k, kindergarten and the early grades.* New America Foundation. Retrieved from https://static.newamerica.org/attachments/2348-getting-in-sync/Getting%20in%20Sync-%20Revamping%20Licensing%20and%20Preparation%20for%20Teachers%20in%20Pre-K%20Kindergarten%20and%20the%20Early%20Grades.e9be94a875084fa5b66a76f858d51a8c.pdf

Bornfreund, L. (2012). Preparing teachers for the early grades. *Educational Leadership*, 69(8), 36–40.

Bredekamp, S. (1987). *Developmentally appropriate practice in early childhood programs serving children from birth though age 8* (expanded ed.). Washington, DC: NAEYC.

Brown, K.C., Squires, J., Connors-Tadros, L., & Horowitz, M. (2014). *Preparing principals to work with early childhood teachers (CEELO FastFact).* New Brunswick, NJ: Center on Enhancing Early Learning Outcomes.

Calder, J. (2014). Early childhood education investment brings big results. *Montana Business Quarterly*, 52(2), 18–20.

Connor, C., Morrison, F., Fishman, B., Giuliani, S., Luck, M., Underwood, P., & Schatschneider, C. (2011). Testing the impact of child characteristics × instruction interactions on third graders' reading comprehension by differentiating literacy instruction. *Reading Research Quarterly*, 46(3), 189–221.

Copple, C., & Bredekamp, S. (Eds.). (2009). *Developmentally appropriate practice in the early childhood programs serving children from birth through age 8.* Washington, DC: National Association for the Education of Young Children.

Copple, C., Bredekamp, S., Koralek, D., & Charner, K. (Eds.). (2014). *Developmentally appropriate practice: Focus on children in first, second, and third grades.* Washington, DC: National Association for the Education of Young Children.

Darling-Hammond, L. (1999). Educating teachers: The academy's greatest failure or its most important future? *Academe*, 85(1), 26–33. doi:10.2307/40251715

Dewey, John. (1916). *Democracy in education*. Wilder, KY: Wilder Publications.

Göncü, A., Main, C., Perone, A., & Tozer, S. (2012, November). *Crossing the boundaries: The need to integrate school leadership and early childhood education* (Policy Brief vol. 1, book 2). Retrieved from http://www.scribd.com/doc/114772928/RUEPI-Crossing-the-Boundaries

Hallissey, M. (2017). *An examination of principals' leadership and its impact on early elementary grades*. Doctoral dissertation, Southern Illinois University at Carbondale. Retrieved from ProQuest Digital Dissertations.

Harris, A.C. (1986). *Child development*. St. Paul, MN: West.

Harrist, A.W., Thompson, S.D., & Norris, D.J. (2007). Defining quality child care: Multiple stakeholder perspectives. *Early Education and Development, 18*(2), 305–336.

Hill, P. (1908). The value and limitations of Froebel's gifts as educative materials Parts I, II. *Elementary School Teacher, 9*(3), 129–137. Retrieved from http://www.jstor.org/stable/992761

Hill, P.S. (1913). *The kindergarten*. Boston, MA: Association for Childhood Education International.

Institute of Medicine (IOM) & National Research Council (NRC). (2015). *Transforming the workforce for children birth through age 8: A unifying foundation*. Washington, DC: The National Academies Press.

Kearns, L. (2011). High-stakes standardized testing and marginalized youth: An examination of the impact on those who fail. *Canadian Journal of Education, 2*, 112–130.

Konecki, L.R., & Schiller, E. (2003). *Brain-based learning and standards-based elementary science*. Grand Rapids, MI: School of Education, Grand Valley State University.

Kostelnik, M., & Grady, M. (2009). *Getting it right from the start*. Thousand Oaks, CA: Sage.

Krusi, H., Karst, J., Spiegle, C., & Korzenik, D. (1875). *Pestallozzi: His life, work and influence*. New York: Van Antwerp, Bragg & Co.

Lacoe, J. (2016). Too scared to learn? The academic consequences of feeling unsafe in the classroom. *Urban Education*. doi:10.1177/0042085916674059

Land, G., & Jarman, B. (1992). *Breakpoint and beyond: Mastering the future today*. Champaign, IL: Harperbusiness.

Mead, S. (2011, April). *PreK–3rd: Principals as crucial instructional leaders*. (Policy to Action Brief No. 7). Foundation for Child Development. Retrieved from http://fed-us.org/resources/prek-3rd-principals-crucial-instructional-leaders

Milkie, M.A., & Warner, C.H. (2011). Classroom learning environments and the mental health of first grade children. *Journal of Health and Social Behavior*, 37, 293–310.

Montessori, M. (1966). *The secret of childhood*. New York: Ballantine.

National Association for the Education of Young Children. (2015). *State profiles*. Retrieved from http://www.naeyc.org/policy/state-profiles

National Policy Board for Educational Administration. (2015). *Professional standards for educational leaders 2015*. Reston, VA: Author.

Robert Wood Johnson Foundation. (2010). *The state of play: A Gallup survey of principals on school recess*. San Francisco, CA: Fenton.

Rudnitski, R.A. (1995). Patty Smith Hill, gifted early childhood educator of the Progressive Era. *Roeper Review*, 18(1), 19–24.

Segool, N.K., Carlson, J.S., Goforth, A.N., von der Embse, N., & Barterian, J.A. (2013). Heightened test anxiety among young children: Elementary school students' anxious responses to high-stakes testing. *Psychology in the Schools*, 50(5), 489–499.

Szekely, A. (2013, May). *Leading for early success: Building school principals' capacity to lead high-quality early education*. Washington, DC: National Governors Association.

Teacher Leadership Exploratory Consortium. (2011). *Teacher leader model standards*. National Education Association.

# CHAPTER TWELVE

# FROM THE PICKUP LINE TO THE PICKET LINE

## Opt Out's Love-Hate Relationship with Public Schools

Todd McCardle, Elizabeth Currin, and Stephanie Schroeder

> *"Everyone preaches that our children are our future, but all we are teaching them is to hate school and that no matter how hard you work, if you can't pass a test, you fail."*
>
> —Opt Out Member

EVERY DAY, PARENTS AND guardians trust that America's teachers and administrators will take good care of their children until the final school bell. This relationship functions in part because parents once sat in classroom desks themselves, but when their children's experiences are disturbingly different from their own, the gap between home and school becomes too pronounced to ignore. As was the case when we were schoolchildren, today's students often step off the bus or approach the pickup line to greet parents or guardians who ask them, "How was your day?" Answers vary from the excited ramblings of primary school students to the shrugging reticence of adolescents, but parents have recently encountered a frightening alternative.

Imagine sending your child to an institution you cannot recognize. Imagine the inordinate amount of little Janie's time spent on high-stakes standardized tests. Imagine how Janie's teacher cannot afford for Janie to make too many mistakes. Imagine Janie's sensitivity to that pressure and the anxiety permeating the school. Imagine little hands struggling with computer keyboards under the watchful eyes of exhausted, fretful teachers. Imagine the definitive "rip" of the seal on the test booklet. Imagine the language barring Janie from discussing the test—with the teacher whose job depends on it, the friends with whom she typically makes sense of her world, and the parent who asks daily, "How was school?" Given this oppressive accountability climate, the response cannot possibly be good.

## Introduction

The burgeoning Opt Out movement, comprising parents and other advocates opposing high-stakes standardized tests, is inherently attuned to why kids love (and hate) school. A common purpose uniting diverse Opt Out groups nationwide is a desire to eliminate high-stakes standardized testing and restore teacher autonomy in public schools in order to ensure that school is a place kids love to be. Put simply, if kids loved school, there would be no need for Opt Out. Instead, because kids hate school in recognizable, recurrent ways, the members of Opt Out feel called to action.

As with most protest movements, Opt Out's energies are directed toward a target: in this case, corporate, neoliberal influence in education. If successful, the members note, Opt Out will no longer be necessary. For now, however, Opt Out members' keen sense of school's detrimental qualities in the Age of Accountability catalyzes the group's collective activism, marked by an informed, compassionate approach to educating students. Teachers and administrators, students and fellow parents, policymakers and all other educational stakeholders would do well to consider what motivates Opt Out, which is to say what inspires their dissent with American public schools.

Having researched the Opt Out movement since 2015, we are intrigued by the members' diverse political affinities and inspired by their grassroots parental activism. Over the course of several months, we joined and observed Opt Out Facebook groups, surveyed 200 members, and interviewed 25 willing participants in both one-on-one and focus group settings, listening to their tales of woe and learning from their visions of what school can and should be. As three high school English teachers turned doctoral students, each with our own love-hate relationship with school, we sympathize with the aims of Opt Out and bring that stance into our critical ethnographic research.

Our conversations with participants revealed the typical pathway to Opt Out membership. First, a personal concern at the dinner table drives parents to search for answers. The discovery of Opt Out social media pages connects them to families with similar grievances. Together, their collective outrage transforms into a powerful response for the sake of all children. In short, the Opt Out movement exists because kids hate school, and there is a discernible pattern in their antipathy.

Opt Out adults identify three main reasons why children hate school: the loss of teacher autonomy, the proliferation of developmentally inappropriate practices, and a narrowing of the curriculum, all of which are symptoms of high-stakes testing. Of course, children feel these trends in more palpable ways, including test-induced stress headaches, gastrointestinal distress, and increased anxiety. Indeed, this is how we know kids hate school, and their guardians in the Opt Out movement have helped us pinpoint the likely culprits of such physical anguish. Insights from Opt Out about why kids hate school, coupled with the movement's implicit critique of neoliberal accountability structures, point to more democratic solutions. Our work with Opt Out has encouraged us to seek transformation in education so that we might all love school.

## Something's Amiss: How Opt Out Knows That Kids Hate School

Bar none, parents joined Opt Out because of the physical and mental stress their children underwent as a result of high-stakes testing. Many shared stories of how their children once loved going to school, but, as a result of "all the tests and exams" now required, kids have come to resent school's "toxic environment." Parents also reported notable alterations in the mental conditions of their children, who suffered from "beyond reasonable" anxiety and even depression, stemming from the "constant threat" of failing a grade or disappointing their teachers.

The mental toll some children were under manifested in physical ailments as well. According to their parents, kids of all ages complained about everything from headaches and stomachaches to vomiting and "wetting their pants." One father urged his wife to take their son to the local hospital because of a recurring stomachache. The parents said the physical pain stopped immediately after telling the child he no longer had to sit for a test.

Teachers in the Opt Out movement also reported how "horrified" they were with testing's detrimental impact on their students. One said her students were afraid to answer questions for fear that they may not have the correct answer, which could "deprive them of opportunities to choose electives." Another said she had six-year-old children who cried when she put a test in front of them.

When considering why kids have come to resent schooling, we cannot ignore the mental and physical stress associated with high-stakes testing. As one parent said: "My kid should not be carrying the weight of the funding for the school, the school's grade, the teacher's evaluation. That isn't on my son."

## Getting to the Root of the Problem:
## The Corporatization and Privatization of Public Schools

Members of the Opt Out movement, driven first by their personal concern for their own children, have joined a growing number of education activists and international scholars in their rejection of high-stakes standardized testing. Across the globe, the slow creep of neoliberal policy into education has been maligned from the teachers' lounge to the ivory tower. Indeed, neoliberal high-stakes accountability, which places a misguided emphasis on "the test" as the ultimate indicator of performance, has led to the deskilling of the teaching profession characterized by the loss of teacher autonomy, the intensification of teaching and schooling, an increased reliance on developmentally inappropriate practices, and the fragmentation and narrowing of curriculum. The impact of these changes on children has been profoundly negative. It is little wonder why kids hate school.

Understanding the source of Opt Out's energy warrants a discussion of the neoliberal climate at the root of students' struggles. A political and economic theory that favors entrepreneurship and free-market capitalism promoted through public or state-run institutions, neoliberalism is nonpartisan and pervasive (Steger & Roy, 2010). Politicians of all stripes can and do promote the values of individualism and competition inherent in neoliberal ideology. Parents and teachers may not know neoliberalism by name, but they readily recognize its manifestations in schools: the increase in standardized assessments, scripted curricula packaged and sold by corporations, school grading systems, and teacher evaluations based on student test scores.

Standardization is a key component of neoliberal ideology: individuals must perform to reach numerical markers used for "comparisons, judgments, and self-management" (Ball, 2013, p. 137). Neoliberal reforms have thus removed the skill from teaching and forced the largely female workforce to adopt rote methods and strategies, otherwise known as "teaching to the test." As these teaching methods fail, teachers are punished and blamed, public schools are shuttered, and school choice in the form of charter schools and voucher programs becomes an attractive alternative. When children react negatively to these components of the neoliberal schooling environment, the parents of Opt Out bear worried witness.

Ending high-stakes accountability measures, according to members in the Opt Out movement, would successfully "deny the data that fuels the machine of privatization" and "stop the corporate takeover of public education." The sole purpose of privatization and corporation, members noted, is "to profit off the backs of our children, teachers, and public schools" using tests that are "not appropriate in either content or development." In fact, as several parents in the movement suggest, the corporations that design the tests stand to benefit financially from students' failure, as they are the ones who have monopolized the scripted remediation curriculum used in many schools. "It's all for the sake of money," a parent said.

Members want to see school accountability and retention policy decisions made at the district and even classroom levels. Staunchly opposing high-stakes tests, especially those related to teacher evaluations, school grades, and school funding, they feel that testing decisions "should be made by the teachers of the class." In order for this to happen, there must be more public awareness of "the damage that testing is doing to education." Public involvement is crucial in "turning the tide" and realizing this goal. This is the gap the Opt Out movement seeks to fill.

### "They're Just Puppets in the Classroom": Teachers' Loss of Autonomy

Since at least the 1970s, scholars have used the term "deskilling" to describe "an imposed loss or degeneration of skills" caused by the teacher's "lack of decision-making power, or lack of use of his/her embodied, situated knowledge" (Chakraborty, 2013, pp. 2–3). In a deskilled classroom, the teacher loses the autonomy of a skilled professional and instead completes tasks that have been divided into small, "standardized units...for managerial control and coordination" (p. 3). In an embattled profession that has historically fought for both autonomy and "professional" status (Goldstein, 2014), the deskilling of teaching has frustrated teacher efforts to maintain "control over their own labor" (Apple & Jungck, 1990, p. 229) and put into practice skills honed over the course of their careers. Instead, teachers become "dispensers of a curriculum and methodology conceived elsewhere by other agents" (Gandin & De Lima, 2015, p. 667).

Tied to the process of deskilling and marked by an increased number of rote tasks required of teachers, the intensification of schooling has also been escalating in recent decades. Examples of such tasks include "systematic application of tests, reading of the didactic material, completing pupils' performance control charts, class control charts, and so on" (Gandin & De Lima, 2015). According to Apple (1986), "Intensification leads people to 'cut corners' so that only what is 'essential' to the task *immediately* at hand is accomplished" (p. 234). As the work of teachers is deskilled and the work demanded of them increases, "quality is sacrificed for quantity. Getting done is substituted for work well done" (Apple, 1986, p. 235). With new and increased demands, teachers rely on prepackaged curricula and embrace the deskilled nature of their work as a way to cope with intensification (Apple & Jungck, 1990), further perpetuating the deskilled status of the profession.

The loss of teacher autonomy was a particularly salient theme in our conversations with members of Opt Out. Parents readily recognized how different their children's experiences are as compared to their own nostalgia of the way school used to be. Additionally, parents with more than one child noted how conditions had worsened in the intervening years from one 3rd-grade experience to the next. Parents were also intuitively aware of dramatic changes within their individual children. As teachers' loss of autonomy increased, so did children's hatred of school.

One mother recalled that "preschool was wonderful" because in early childhood education, "they learn through play, and it's the process—not product—that's important." She described her child's pleasant experience as "screeching to a halt" in kindergarten, finding solace among parents with similar stories. Significantly, these tales evoke a sense that conditions have changed. Another parent concurred, saying she witnessed how "the testing pressure has changed the way teachers can teach," which concurrently led to a "less well-rounded" experience for schoolchildren and "more stress for teachers and students." Several mothers echoed the sentiment of wanting to "give power back to the local districts," returning "trust to the teachers," and allowing teachers to "go back to actually enjoying their jobs."

Some members gave a name to this change: deprofessionalization, which creates an atmosphere in which anyone can teach but no one really wants to. One member explained:

> They've always had guidelines, and you know, these are profes-
> sionals and they've been trained and have four-year degrees, many
> masters' degrees, and some even with doctoral degrees, so these are
> educated people, but yet we're spoon-feeding and asking them to
> be puppets, which is insulting. So, teachers know how to get the job
> done. We need to let them do it and do it in the best way they can
> and know how.

Instead of the autonomous scenario this parent imagines, deskilling of the profession has simultaneously deprived educators of trust, though many have more than a decade of teaching experience. Opt Out members consistently perceived that "teachers [were] being spoon-fed," leading one parent to point out that the removal of trust is unique to education. "You don't do that to a doctor. You don't do that to a lawyer, to a policeman. You don't do it to other professions."

To combat the deprofessionalization of teachers caused by accountability measures, several mothers urged policymakers to trust the teachers to "do what they are hired to do and what they've trained to do in the classroom." Indeed, Opt Out members wished to have teachers "treated as professionals" with the ability to make assessment decisions in their classrooms, decisions they were trained to make in their degree programs. Instead, many members feel that teachers are merely reduced to serving as "puppets in the classroom," and they point to this as ample evidence for why their kids hate school.

## "Putting Shackles on Our Best and Brightest": Developmentally Inappropriate Practice

The deskilling and intensification of teaching has led to the increased use of developmentally inappropriate practices in education. Basal readers and other pre-scripted curriculum materials have been under siege for decades as standing "at odds with the principles of developmentally appropriate practice" (Crawford, 2004, p. 205). Developmentally appropriate practice (DAP), as defined by the National Association for the Education of Young Children, "refers to a child-centered approach to instruction" that "recognizes young children's unique characteristics" (Charlesworth, 1998, p. 275). It is inherently non-standard, as DAP "views the child as the primary source of the curriculum" (p. 275). Conversely, developmentally inappropriate practice (DIP) does not pay attention to "individual differences, and assessment focuses on weekly quizzes, end-of-unit tests and standardized test scores" (p. 275). Worksheets, rote practice, and memorization characterize instruction, with little attention to "hands-on, concrete experiences" (p. 275). Despite guidelines warning against the infusion of DIP into early childhood education due to its association with increased stress behaviors in children (Burts, Hart, Charlesworth, & Kirk, 1990; Jackson, 2009), Stipek (2006) cites concerns that early childhood education is not immune to the Age of Accountability. Indeed, parents of young children are at the forefront of the Opt Out movement, often decrying the developmentally inappropriate nature of high-stakes tests.

Opt Out parents pointed to the ill-designed tools used to assess their children, especially children with special needs and those in the early years of schooling. They felt the schools placed "shackles" on their children, making them "feel stupid" because they did not test well. One parent warned that schools are "labeling and condemning" children at age 6, an age where "they can barely hold a pencil." Children with special needs, a population all too familiar with the impact of labeling, prompted particular concern: "Their parents know [their children] are not performing on grade level," one parent said. "I don't see the point in slapping the children and slapping their parents in the face by giving them a test that's not appropriate for them."

Another parent, voicing her concern that testing has eroded her child's love of learning and the development of her creativity and critical thinking skills, asserted that high-stakes tests are not administered to evaluate student progress. Their purpose, she said, is to "further erode the professionalism of teachers and to damage support for public education." In this manner, the reasons why kids hate school are inextricably connected as elements of the larger neoliberal climate.

As testament to that oppressive milieu, an Opt Out member recognized the amount of homework assigned to kindergartners in her community. She noted seeing them completing multiple pages of assigned worksheets in the local library because their families do not have internet access at home. Furthermore, the students have no choice but to work alone "because their parents don't understand what they are doing."

A teacher in Opt Out clarified that the movement is not against raising the rigor of teaching and learning in the schools. In fact, she said, "there should be some level of standards." The common misconception stems from a conflation of rigor and intensification. In this teacher's view, "[teachers] love kids" and want to see them grow in the face of developmentally appropriate challenges. However, "this psycho testing going on" impedes teachers' ability to organize rigorous learning experiences, further contributing to the reasons why kids hate school.

### "Put the Education Back in the Classroom": Narrowing of the Curriculum

Compounding the loss of teacher autonomy and the developmentally inappropriate nature of schooling, high-stakes testing also largely determines what gets taught and how. In essence, whoever controls the high stakes controls the curriculum, reasserting policymakers' power over teachers and teachers' power over students. High-stakes testing strongly correlates with teacher-centered instruction, such that over time, knowledge becomes increasingly fragmented, and pacing guides strictly align with tests, ignoring important non-tested subjects (Au, 2007).

When this narrowing of the curriculum is in force, schools not only marginalize subjects; they also marginalize students whose interests are outside of core knowledge areas (Eisner, 2001). Even within core subjects, as more high-stakes measures are adopted, teachers are less likely to teach in rich, integrated ways; instead, they tend to value isolated facts over critical thinking skills (Au, 2007). They also opt to select traditional texts over multicultural literature (Sleeter & Stillman, 2005). This pernicious problem reinforces established power structures and teachers' and students' subordinate places within those hierarchies.

Rather than resulting in laudable and lasting educational change, accountability policies prompt teachers to ignore their "responsibility for the intellectual development of their students" and answer instead to higher powers up the administrative hierarchical chain who "demand for higher test scores" (Noddings, 2009, p. 19). The pressure teachers face from administrators to "deliver instruction on a tightly prescribed curriculum" precludes "permanent or long-lasting learning" and hinders teachers' ability to "respond to the legitimate needs" of the students in their classrooms (Noddings, 2009, pp. 17, 19–20). When tied to grade-level promotion, performance on high-stakes assessments becomes an alarming substitute for authentic education.

Parents feel the schooling their children receive as a result of teachers' "teaching to the test" is "no longer of any quality." One parent, who said her children attend one of the top schools in the state, claimed that class time is "wasted" preparing students to be test takers. She felt her children's education is too important for her to "allow anyone to treat them as guinea pigs." Inauthentic learning also affects the curriculum outside of the mandated testing dates. A mother in Opt Out pointed to the lack of academic rigor in the weeks following testing. She said, "Since testing ended, they do nothing in school." Instead of focusing on the curriculum, the teachers have the students "watch movies, go bowling, and play dodge ball against the teachers." Indeed, Opt Out parents advocate to "put the education back into the classroom."

Teachers, however, are placed in a difficult position as a result of high-stakes standardized testing. One parent claimed that "testing is taking away the ability of teachers to create interesting and engaging classrooms." In this Age of Accountability, many teachers feel they must remain obedient to the rules associated with state-mandated testing. Understanding this predicament, a public school employee who participated in our study warned that teachers who do not adequately follow testing procedures "could lose [their] certification."

The narrowing of the curriculum associated with teaching to the test thus impacts teachers and students alike, with noticeable ramifications for electives and non-tested subjects. Students who either opt out or do not pass these tests are at risk of alternative curricular placements for the following school year if not outright retention. One parent voiced her fear of her child being "penalized" for opting out. Her school, she claimed, placed children who opt out or do not pass in remedial courses that occupy multiple blocks during the school day. She claimed that this would cause her daughter to miss out on either a gym or an art class. Another parent who lived this reality said her daughter was enrolled in an intensive reading class based on her lack of test scores. The teacher told her that her daughter was misplaced and should not be in that class, but the school required she remain because of its policy regarding the state test scores. With such procedures in place, and such high stakes on the line, it is little wonder why kids hate school.

**"This is a social justice issue": Parents Strike Back with Potential Solutions**
Parents are all too often excluded from conversations about school, particularly of the scholarly variety. We recognize their powerful, perspicacious voices, as well as their earnest desire to speak on behalf of teachers and students who feel institutionally silenced (Schroeder, Currin, & McCardle, 2016). As one mother passionately proclaimed, "Teachers have been de-professionalized and demoralized, [...] young children are expected to learn concepts far beyond what is developmentally appropriate, and when they 'fail' the almighty test, fingers are pointed at the teachers who are accused of being incompetent." We agree that "It's sickening what has happened to public education," and we also share Opt Out's enthusiasm for finding a remedy and returning "our public schools back to the hands of the public."

"We're about reclaiming our public schools, not abandoning them," declares the Opt Out Florida Network's website. As critical ethnographers celebrating our participants' ability to empower themselves in the face of injustice, we hope to communicate this message above all others: the parents of Opt Out have mobilized from the pickup line to the picket line because at its core, the movement was born of a deep love for the potential of American schools and the students and teachers within them.

Our participants' concern for teachers is worth reiterating, given some scholars' tendency to place the blame for problems in education squarely at teachers' feet. Strickland (1998) documents patterns of children's physical discomfort at school as resulting from demonstrably bad teachers; Opt Out, on the other hand, compassionately acknowledges teachers' distress in the face of the same forces that harm their students. Simultaneously criticized and held up as the most critical factors in a child's education, teachers in the Age of Accountability occupy an especially precarious position (Cochran-Smith, 2015; Kumashiro, 2012). Opt Out recognizes that kids hate school—and goes one step further to wonder if teachers do, too.

For Kohn (1999), who readily endorses test boycotts, moving past the Age of Accountability means envisioning "a kind of education that is fundamentally about democracy—not as a vague political goal but as a commitment to giving people (including young people) more say about what happens to them every day" (p. 185). By staying attuned to their children's lived experiences, maintaining empathy for teachers, and engaging in crucial social activism, the parents of Opt Out are ably positioned to usher in the kind of learning environment Kohn and other public school advocates imagine.

What alternatives to neoliberal, high-stakes accountability exist? For the parents in the Opt Out movement, this is "a social justice issue," and the first step to imagining a post-neoliberal education system is to educate more parents on the dangers of the corporatization of public schools and then "encourage those with kids that attend public schools to opt out and starve the data...that fuels the [corporate] beast." One member shared her hope to "raise awareness and encourage dialogue about the over testing of our students and the unfair policies based on test scores." Many also point to urging their state congressional representatives to enact "comprehensive legislative solutions addressing the role of for-profit corporate entities in education and mandating a return to humanizing practices within the field of education." Some members underscore that assessment and testing are an important part of the education process and "have a place" in our public schools, but "they are not, by any means, sufficient for sole determination of a child's academic capabilities, or teachers' educational skills." Members desire for teaching and learning to regain respect rather than remaining "just a set of quantifiable outcomes." For now, Opt Out members vow to continue to fight the misuse of assessments in the Age of Accountability and "restore the dignity" of all the little Janies "who are being treated as data points, rather than living and learning children."

## References

Apple, M. (1986). *Teachers and texts: A political economy of class and gender relations in education.* New York: Routledge.

Apple, M., & Jungck, S. (1990). "You don't have to be a teacher to teach this unit": Teaching, technology, and gender in the classroom. *American Educational Research Journal, 27*(2), 227–251.

Au, W. (2007). High-stakes testing and curricular control: A qualitative metasynthesis. *Educational Researcher, 36*(5), 258–267.

Ball, S.J. (Ed.). (2013). *Foucault and education: Disciplines and knowledge*. New York: Routledge.

Burts, D.C., Hart, C.H., Charlesworth, R., & Kirk, L. (1990). A comparison of frequencies of stress behaviors observed in kindergarten children in classrooms with developmentally appropriate versus developmentally inappropriate instructional practices. *Early Childhood Research Quarterly*, 5(3), 407–423.

Chakraborty, S. (2013). Deskilling of the teaching profession. In J. Ainsworth (Ed.), *Sociology of education: An A to Z guide* (pp. 184–186). Los Angeles: Sage Publications.

Charlesworth, R. (1998). Developmentally appropriate practice is for everyone. *Childhood Education*, 74(5), 274–281.

Cochran-Smith, M. (2015). A tale of two teachers: Learning to teach over time. *LEARNing Landscapes*, 8(2), 111–134.

Crawford, P.A. (2004). "I follow the blue…" A primary teacher and the impact of packaged curricula. *Early Childhood Education Journal*, 32(3), 205–210.

Eisner, E.W. (2001). *The educational imagination: On design and evaluation of school programs* (5th ed.). Upper Saddle River, NJ: Prentice Hall.

Gandin, L.A., & De Lima, I.G. (2015). Reconfiguration of teacher's work: An examination of the introduction of pedagogical intervention programs. *Revista Brasileira de Educação*, 20(62), 663–677.

Goldstein, D. (2014). *The teacher wars: A history of America's most embattled profession*. New York: Anchor.

Jackson, L.A. (2009). Observing children's stress behaviors in a kindergarten classroom. *Early Childhood Research & Practice*, 11(1). Retrieved from https://files.eric.ed.gov/fulltext/EJ848845.pdf

Kohn, A. (1999). *The schools our children deserve: Moving beyond traditional classrooms and "tougher standards."* Boston: Houghton Mifflin.

Kumashiro, K.K. (2012). *Bad teacher: How blaming teachers distorts the bigger picture*. New York: Teachers College Press.

Noddings, N. (2009). Commentary: Responsibility. *LEARNing Landscapes*, 2(2), 17–23.

Schroeder, S., Currin, E., & McCardle, T. (2016). Mother tongues: The Opt Out movement's vocal response to patriarchal, neoliberal education reform. *Gender and Education*, 1–18. Retrieved from doi: 10.1080/09540253.2016.1270422

Sleeter, C., & Stillman, J. (2005). Standardizing knowledge in a multicultural society. *Curriculum Inquiry*, 35(1), 27–46.

Steger, M.B., & Roy, R.K. (2010). *Neoliberalism: A very short introduction*. New York: Oxford University Press.

Stipek, D. (2006). Accountability comes to preschool: Can we make it work for young children? *Phi Delta Kappan*, 87(10), 740–747.

Strickland, G. (1998). *Bad teachers: The essential guide for concerned parents*. New York: Pocket Books.

**Christopher Beckham** is Assistant Professor of Education at Morehead State University, Morehead, Kentucky, where he teaches courses in the history and philosophy of education. He is an advocate for the use of core texts (or "the great books," as they are sometimes called) in teacher education. His recent historical research has resulted in several presentations and a publication on the educational activities of Protestant reformer Martin Luther.

**Elizabeth Currin** is a former high school English teacher and current doctoral candidate in Curriculum, Teaching, and Teacher Education at the University of Florida. Her research interests include practitioner inquiry, the sociological and historical foundations of education, and representations of schools in pop culture.

**Kari Dahle-Huff** is Assistant Professor of Reading at Montana State University, Billings. She is also the Institutional Coordinator for the Peace Corps Prep certificate program and was herself a Peace Corps volunteer in the Republic of Georgia. She earned her Ph.D. from the University of Minnesota. Her research interests include critical literacy, place-conscious education, and community reading intervention programs. She is an avid hiker in the Montana mountains with her family.

**James Davis** is a professor and program coordinator in Educational Leadership at Coastal Carolina University. He received his doctorate from the University of North Carolina at Charlotte in Curriculum and Instruction, with a focus on Urban Education. Prior to his positions at the university level, he served as a school transformation principal. His research interests include school transformation, teacher effectiveness, teacher leadership, principal support, and serving at-risk populations.

**Megan Hallissey** received her Bachelor's degree in Theater from Northwestern University, her Master's degree in Education from DePaul University, and her interdisciplinary Ph.D. from Southern Illinois University in Early Childhood Education and Educational Administration. With over 20 years of teaching experience, she regularly presents at local, state, and national conferences. Dr. Hallissey's research endeavors include the need for more transformative teaching practices, including arts integration and developmentally appropriate practices for middle grades education.

**Elizabeth Hobbs** is a devoted dog lover, lifelong Iowa Hawkeye, insatiable news junkie—and a lover of poetic justice, peaceful beaches, profound books, and perfect cups of coffee. Dr. Hobbs currently teaches English at Neuqua Valley High School in Naperville, Illinois, and moonlights as an adjunct education professor at Aurora University in Aurora, Illinois. At the end of the day, she hopes her students leave her classroom ever empowered to be kind and brave.

**Gary Homana** is Assistant Professor in the College of Education at Towson University. His research interests include the social organization of classrooms and schools. He is particularly interested in the intersection of civic literacy and engagement, communities of practice, service-learning, and school climate for improved teaching and learning. He is executive producer of *Voices of Baltimore: Life under Segregation*, a documentary film that preserves the narratives of individuals who lived through segregation/desegregation.

**Steven P. Jones** is a professor in the College of Education at Missouri State University and Executive Director of the Academy for Educational Studies. He is the author of *Blame Teachers: The Emotional Reasons for Educational Reform*, a book that investigates how and why people deride the efforts and effectiveness of our public school teachers. A former high school English teacher, he received his B.A. in English from the University of Denver, his M.A. in Educational Administration from the University of Colorado (Boulder), and his Ph.D. in Curriculum and Instruction from the University of Chicago.

**Irene S. LaRoche** is a social studies teacher at Amherst Regional Middle School in Amherst, Massachusetts. She is co-author with Robert W. Maloy of *We, the Students and Teachers: Teaching Democratically in the History and Social Studies Classroom* (State University of New York Press, 2015). Her current research focuses on the use of student feedback surveys and democratic teaching strategies in social studies classrooms.

**Barbara J. Mallory** is Associate Professor and program coordinator for the doctoral program in educational leadership at High Point University. Prior to her career in higher education, Dr. Mallory served as a high school principal and worked as a district and school transformation team leader for the North Carolina Department of Public Instruction. Her research interests include principal coaching, principal support, and similarities and differences in school leadership from a global perspective.

**Robert W. Maloy** is Senior Lecturer in the Department of Teacher Education and Curriculum Studies in the College of Education at the University of Massachusetts Amherst. He coordinates the university history and political science teacher license programs and co-directs the College of Education's TEAMS Tutoring Project. He is co-author of several books, including *Wiki Works: Teaching Web Research and Digital Literacy in the History and Humanities Classroom* (Rowman & Littlefield, 2017). He also serves as webmaster for the *resourcesforhistoryteachers* wiki.

**Todd McCardle** is Assistant Professor of Curriculum and Instruction at Eastern Kentucky University. His research interests include the roles of diversity and issues of social justice in public schools and teacher education programs. He earned a Ph.D. in Curriculum and Instruction in 2017 from the University of Florida.

**Barbara J. Rose** is Associate Professor of Teacher Education at Miami University. Her teaching and scholarship focus is on social justice, educational equity, and student writing. She teaches introduction to education, advanced writing for educators, and a senior capstone, and previously taught courses on dominant privilege, the cultural context of integrity, and other topics. Recent and upcoming publications are in the *Currere Exchange Journal* (2017 and 2018), *Brock Education Journal* (2017), and *The Educational Forum* (2018).

**Stephanie Schroeder** is an Assistant Professor of Elementary Social Studies Education at Pennsylvania State University. Her research interests include democratic and citizenship education, preservice teacher education, and social studies education. She earned a Ph.D. in curriculum, teaching, and teacher education in 2018 from the University of Florida.

**Eric C. Sheffield** is Professor and Department Chair of Educational Studies at Western Illinois University in Macomb. He is also the founding editor of the Academy for Educational Studies' peer-reviewed journal, *Critical Questions in Education*. A former English teacher in Putnam County, Florida, Sheffield received his B.A. in Philosophy from Illinois College and his M.Ed. and Ph.D. from the University of Florida.

**Karla Smart-Morstad,** Professor Emerita of Education at Concordia College, Moorhead, Minnesota, remains active as a qualitative researcher. While at Concordia, Dr. Smart-Morstad taught secondary teacher education students in English methods, reading across the curriculum, social foundations, and comparative education courses. Travel seminars with students to Scandinavia and northern Europe brought colleagueship and research opportunities with teachers and administrators from Denmark and Iceland.

**Megan J. Sulsberger** is Assistant Professor in the Department of Education and Leadership at California State University, Monterey Bay. She received a Ph.D. in Curriculum and Instruction with a focus on Science Education from Virginia Polytechnic Institute and State University. She teaches math and science methods and is the lead on two STEM Teacher grants. Her research interests include STEM education, environmental education, teacher identity, teacher preparation, and the intersection of these topics.

**Sara B. Triggs,** Associate Professor of Education at Concordia College, Moorhead, Minnesota, teaches elementary science methods and social foundations. She has published qualitative research on homelessness in education, student choice in elementary curricula, and descriptive review of children's art. Dr. Triggs involves her students with public school classrooms through STEM inquiry projects. Addressing social justice issues for teachers and the students and families they serve is a priority for her teaching and research.

**Liang Zhao** currently lives in China. At the time this book was being put together, Liang was a faculty member at St. Xavier University in Chicago. An active researcher and educational thinker, Liang studied American education carefully and took a special interest in books by Rafe Esquith—finding a liveliness in the teaching approaches taken by Esquith that he had never seen used by teachers in China.